In Search of Trout

In Search of

TROUT

by

PETER BARRETT

PRENTICE-HALL, *Inc., Englewood Cliffs, New Jersey*

The following chapters are reprinted by permission of Fawcett Publications, Inc.: Chapter 5 originally appeared as "The Strangest Trout Lake" in *True's Fishing Yearbook, No. 9,* © 1958 by Fawcett Publications, Inc.; Chapter 8 originally appeared as "River of Gorging Trout" in *True's Fishing Yearbook, No. 13,* © 1962 by Fawcett Publications, Inc.; Chapter 10 originally appeared as "Two Miles of Trout" in *True,* April, 1960, © 1960 by Fawcett Publications, Inc.; Chapter 11 originally appeared as "The Lake that Turns Fish Stories into Fact" in *True,* April, 1964, © 1964 by Fawcett Publications, Inc.

Chapter 4 originally appeared as "A Return to the Roaring Kill" in *Field & Stream* magazine, May, 1971.

The following are reprinted from *Outdoor Life* magazine, Popular Science Publishing Co., Inc.: Chapter 1 originally appeared as "Casting's Fun, But Can You Catch Trout?", March 1963; Chapter 2 originally appeared as "Don't Stay Dry," October, 1957; Chapter 3 originally appeared as "How to Fool April Trout," April, 1969; Chapter 6 originally appeared as "The Amazing Method," June, 1959; Chapter 7 originally appeared as "Toughest Lake," November, 1957; Chapter 9 originally appeared as "Trout that Never Hear Traffic," June, 1966.

Library of Congress Cataloging in Publication Data
Barrett, Peter.
  In search of trout.

  1. Trout fishing.   I. Title.
SH687.B374   799.1'7'55   73-7544
ISBN 0-13-453845-5

10 9 8 7 6 5 4 3 2 1

PREFACE

MOST SUCCESSFUL fly fishermen were once *bait* fishermen, though they don't usually admit this. When a person starts fishing at an early age, live bait is an easy way to get started because it is effective even when the user is unskilled, and also because it is a great teacher. The beginner who starts fishing for trout with bait quickly learns more about the habits and lies of his quarry than does someone who starts an angling career with flies.

For this reason—though *In Search of Trout* is mainly about fly fishing—there are three chapters about using live bait. For I believe that if a person is to be really grounded in the ways of trout, bait fishing is the logical first step toward fly fishing. In addition, fishing natural bait like a worm can be downright fun. I still do it once every spring with two old friends with whom I fished worms when we were kids.

Let us not forget that fly fishing is nothing more than bait fishing with artificial substitutes for the real thing.

After an angler has begun to catch trout on flies, has advanced beyond casting in a manner which the British wryly label "Chuck and chance it," then another goal looms. Call it "difficult trout." You are in a situation where you know there are fish but you can't catch them. Not at first, anyway.

There are some difficult trout everywhere. Learning how to catch them on flies becomes a challenge wherein lies the fascination of the game. I hope this book will help beginning trout fishermen succeed in their challenges.

PETER BARRETT

CONTENTS

INTRODUCTION

IT WAS A HOT, sticky August afternoon before World War II and I was fishing the Ten Mile River in Dutchess County, New York, with a skinny little guy I hadn't known long. He handled a fly rod as naturally as a dog wags its tail and he seemed to have a superhuman ability to put the fly right where an eager trout was waiting for it.

I waded along, methodically covering the water and making what seemed like 5,000 casts for every strike—and that usually from a chub—but my companion would walk the bank for 100 yards or so, step in, make a cast, let his line sink and then, as it swung around in the current, work his sparsely dressed wet fly back with a slow, hand-twist retrieve. He got a strike nearly every time, and sometimes landed two or three trout in one spot.

I had recently come from the West, where the water is always cold, and I was baffled by the too-warm river and the lethargic trout. Finally I asked Peter Barrett what his secret was.

Just ahead, the inviting shade of a huge sycamore was beginning to lengthen out across the river. We walked on to this welcome refuge from the sun, sat down beside the bank, and pulled down our waders to cool our steaming legs. Pete took a vacuum bottle from the back of his fishing vest and poured us each a cup of the great iced tea his mother used to make when we went fishing—strong and black, with a bit of sugar and the juice of a whole lemon to the quart. As we drank our tea, Pete said,

"There were trout everywhere along here in June, remember? Well, a couple of years ago I made up my mind to find out where they went in August. I wore sneakers and waded the whole stretch—back and forth across it—too. Didn't even try to fish. I discovered that a lot of springs come out beneath the surface, oozing up through the gravel. I could feel the cold water on my feet. Obviously when the river is too warm for comfort, the trout will lie in the cool, spring water. I marked each spot well and I've been catching fish from them ever since."

That was more than ten years ago, and it is hard for me to realize that Pete and I have fished together for four decades. In that period Peter Barrett's brown hair has turned gray, he has put on a little weight—and he has learned a great deal more about trout. He has caught them in the Catskills and the Rockies and from many waters in between. If ever there was an angler who could think like a fish, Peter Barrett is that man. The things that he has to say about trout fishing in the following pages deserve your attention.

—TED TRUEBLOOD

I

PROBLEMS OF THE EAST

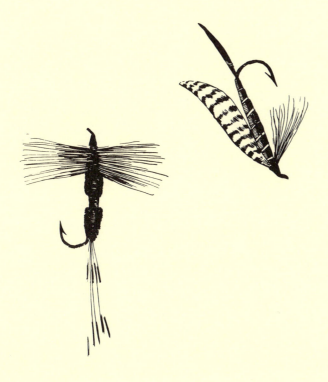

The First Step—

Learn a Local Stream with Bait

THIS BOOK IS mostly about fly fishing for trout with wets, drys, nymphs, and streamers. Yet fly fishing is essentially bait fishing with an artificial substitute, and behind most successful fly fishermen there lies experience with live bait. And so that is how this book begins: By observing how trout react to natural baits.

It is often said that ten percent of all fishermen catch ninety percent of all the trout. For some time now, I've often joined the ranks of the elite ten percent, but it wasn't always so. I'd known entire weekends of despair and hadn't a clue as to what I was doing wrong. I still can have as poor a day as anybody, but if I fail now I usually know why.

A simple thing put me on the track of trout: I learned how to fish a small stream with bait. Pick a little stream with pools, bends, broken water, and some overhanging banks, and you have big-trout water in miniature. But there's one vital difference: In the small stream you can often see the fish.

What an awakener this is if you have been baffled by trout.

I'll never forget my first revealing glimpse of a broad, meadow pool in the stream that I adopted near my home. It was Titicus Outlet in upper Westchester County, New York. In the mid-1930's, Polaroid glasses—those wonderful glare-cutters—had only recently come on the market, and I'd just gotten my first pair. There were trout in the pool, all right, but not where I thought they'd be.

Two 10-inch browns hovered in the shade in a "wrong" part of the pool that was only a foot deep. What were these trout doing in water I'd never have given a second glance before? As I stared, one rose very quietly. Brown trout like shade, I was to learn, when it's available in hours of strong sunlight on the water. This pair had typically stationed themselves in a not-too-fast stretch where the swimming was easy and in a line of current that brought most floating insects on their side of the pool directly over them.

None of this was clear to me then.

I stared hungrily at the two trout and took a step forward to see better. A trout that had been lying practically at my feet near some trailing grass suddenly bolted. It was a brookie or rainbow that went too fast to identify. Its flight spooked the pair of browns and another trout down the pool which I also hadn't noticed.

That day taught me to move slowly when approaching a pool, whether to fish it or just look at it. I found that brown and brook trout prefer seclusion but that rainbows favor more open water and don't mind hanging in a fast current.

Not until I'd spied on the trout for two or three weekends did I stumble onto the fact that a river has certain choice locations where almost invariably a trout or two will hang. Catch a trout from one of these spots and chances are another will have adopted the location a week later. Two such places in Titicus have yielded dozens of trout to me over the years.

One of these was an insignificant-looking pocket near the tail of a shallow pool that was only about fifteen feet long and eight or nine feet wide. Only one trout at a time would occupy this little pool, and eight times out of ten the tenant would be in the pocket—no doubt because most of the pool's food washed through it.

In those days when I couldn't see into a stretch of water to assess it without revealing myself and spooking the trout, I'd throw a wood chip or bit of bark onto the water upstream and watch where the current carried it. After I'd studied the path of two or three chips, I'd have a fair idea whether there were side areas to the main current where trout might lurk.

Except when trout forage actively, which is usually early or late in the day or when there's a

Having learned to fish Titicus Outlet, pool by pool, I drop nymph into aerated water, which holds trout in warm weather.

good hatch on, they lead a rather indolent existence and prefer stations which don't require much
swimming to maintain position.

With my Polaroids and new knowledge of where
some of the fish were, I went after them with
worms, but except for catching a small trout
occasionally, my luck remained poor. It was May,
with water low and quite clear. Now what was
wrong?

A 13-inch rainbow taught me something. I'd
spotted him in an open stretch where I could
observe him well from my casting position. Presently my worm—a small, lively one at the end of a
light leader—was swimming toward him a couple of
inches off the bottom. As the worm passed the
trout by no more than a foot, the rainbow seemed
to tense.

Titicus was like this in 1946.
Now the pines at left are as
tall as spruces on right.

He wants it, I thought.

Soon I made another cast. But instead of the
bait passing the trout, the leader caught on a rock
and the worm came to a halt about two feet above
the fish. Immediately the rainbow turned downstream and took up a new position ten feet away.
It looked warier than ever.

Then I had an inspiration. I took out a fresh
worm and tossed it into the water unhooked. *Plop!*
It went more than a yard above my guinea-pig
trout. The worm floated toward the fish ever so
nicely and passed within range. In fact it stopped
on the bottom barely a foot behind the rainbow
and lay there wriggling enticingly.

Well, I had a whole boxful of worms. I'd just
toss this knothead another. This worm had an even
better drift, and I held my breath as it drew even
with the fish. The rainbow plainly eyed the worm,
but instead of going for it, he changed his position
a yard to one side, as if deliberately avoiding my
worm zone.

Ever so carefully I unhooked my bottom-caught
worm and backed out of position without spooking the trout. I knew where there should be
another fish in the pool above and went directly to
it.

The trout was there. This time I didn't try a
hooked worm but gave it a free one. No interest.
Once again the trout I watched seemed to have an
aware, nervous look.

I withdrew and began searching the bank for any
live thing, besides a worm, to try on my trout. A
turned-over rock revealed a lively hellgrammite
which I grabbed and carried back to the first
rainbow, now that it had had a rest.

My toss was poor; the hellgrammite was going to
miss the rainbow by a yard. I was about to retire
for more bait when the fish suddenly spotted the
tumbling hellgrammite and went after it as if he'd
been waiting all his life for it.

Man! I could hardly contain myself as I backed away. Then I began a frantic search under more bankside rocks. Eventually I uncovered another hellgrammite, inserted the hook point under the collar, pulled it out the other side and made what was to be a momentous cast.

The rainbow actually charged the bait the moment it came wiggling into view. I had the satisfaction of a solidly set hook in a wildly jumping trout. Here was no fish I'd caught by accident. I'd spotted him, tempted his appetite, stalked him, and now I had him. It was a sweet moment. That day I caught four good trout, all with the same bait. And these were sophisticated trout, too. Titicus was close to New York City—so close that the skyscrapers could be seen from the heights just above the lake—and, as a result, it took quite a pounding.

My discovery that educated trout were suspicious of a worm in low, clear water but not of the other natural baits of the streamside or the bottom gave me a great lift.

Experimenting, I found that leeches, caddisfly larvae, and small salamanders (hooked in the forearm) were also effective. I took pains to cast from beside, or a bit below a located trout, lobbing the bait about two yards upstream so as not to alarm it with the splash.

Sometime in this period I became a bank prodder. Titicus, for the most part, is a comparatively shallow stream, and I got to wondering where the trout disappeared when I spooked them. I cut a willow branch and began to probe under rocks and banks with it. The stream was full of surprises. Some insignificant-looking rocks had veritable parking garages for trout under them; others that looked promising were not. I cased the entire stream—it's only about a mile long—in one afternoon.

Pools that offered good fishing usually had one, two, and maybe three such refuges, and now I knew them all. Only one location baffled me, a bend pool that looked trouty but always seemed barren. Probing away, I found a considerable cavern under a smallish rock. How come no trout lived in this pool? I was not to get the answer until we had an August deluge.

Most of the time, Titicus Outlet is fed cold water emitted by a big pipe from the bottom of the lake above. But when the lake was full to overflowing, surface water entered the stream via the dam spillway. Because of the cool water from the outlet pipe the stream offered good fishing all summer, and since it was the inlet of another lake, it frequently attracted trout into its cool reaches.

To learn a stream, probe under big rocks. Some lack room to shelter trout.

But then came a heavy rain, and the stream went over its banks.

I was trying to catch trout on all types of flies, and when I saw how high the stream was, I decided to try a streamer fly. The water was so fast it seemed hopeless, but I kept on.

At length I came to the bend pool with the cavern under the rock. Most of the pool was white water, but there was a dark, not-so-fast spot in front of the rock. I tossed the fly idly onto this dark water and gave the rod a twitch.

As long as I live I'll never forget that trout. He rolled hungrily on the streamer, and I gasped when I got a glimpse of his broad, yellow side. The fish seemed as strong as a bull and I could only humor him, still keeping pressure on the 2X leader.

It seemed hours before I got him netted and on

Grasshoppers sent downstream as trout-finders must be released gently. Tossed in, they sink.

the bank. He was 21 incredible inches of brown trout and had been living a cannibalistic existence under that rock. When the water dropped to normal, two or three lesser trout moved into the pool. Obviously, the old boy had declared the pool his private domain and had either eaten or scared off all smaller, intruding trout.

If you fish a small stream with a mysterious barren area that looks good but isn't—investigate further. But use strong enough tackle.

Knowing these trout hideouts paid off in other ways. When some incautious angler came along and spooked the fish in several pools, I found that if I let them rest for about half an hour, then lowered some choice natural bait in front of the hideaway entrance, I'd often catch a trout.

Fish also use such refuges when high water offers no resting places in the stream proper and in the spring when the water is very cold and the trout sluggish.

One spring in the late 1930's, I struck a real bonanza beneath a rock in a meadow pool. I wasn't surprised when I caught two trout under it. But when a third, a fourth, a fifth, and finally a sixth came eagerly for the bait, I was amazed.

What gave me my next big advantage over the trout of Titicus was the use of a brass Colorado spinner in the two smallest sizes—3/0 and 4/0. Spinning tackle and techniques were unknown in the U.S. then and for those of us who chanced upon the Colorado the reaction of trout to this bit of shiny, revolving hardware came as a shock.

This spinner was also shocking on a windy day; it frequently belted me on the back of the head and sometimes caught an ear. But the Colorado not only caught fish, it also revealed other trout too smart to hit it but too curious to ignore it. This was my big advantage; I used the Colorado as a fish-finder.

You can seldom see all the trout in a pool, even

with Polaroid glasses and favorable watching conditions. Add a cautiously cast Colorado, however, and your score takes an upward leap. Some trout follow the little spinner out of curiosity. Others will give a sort of quiver or two as it passes. But just this slight flash of a trout when you're watching is enough to reveal its presence. I've often heard it said that when trout are rising to flies, it is usually a waste of time to fish for them with other offerings. It is a measure of the Colorado's power of attraction that rising trout will often flash at it, and I've had some risers actually hit it hard.

After I had begun to catch trout with some regularity on flies, I continued to use the Colorado with the treble hook removed as a trout finder. Once I'd spotted a couple of fish this way, I could then try for them with flies. The girl I was showing how to fish in those days used to think I was some kind of genius because I seemed to know exactly where the trout were. I knew this because on the previous evenings, I'd made it a practice to check the stream with a hookless Colorado.

My biggest problem in Titicus was learning how to catch trout on wet flies and nymphs. I'd taken up fly tying as a means of saving money and in an attempt to match some of the creatures I found in the stream under rocks—May-fly nymphs, hellgrammites, and the like.

A hellgrammite was the first nymph I tried, and I made the mistake of trying to copy it exactly. Then an unfortunate thing happened. I caught a nine-inch brook trout with the nymph on the very first cast. I saw it all clearly—the hovering trout, the approaching nymph, and the sudden, eager strike. I thought I was going to catch every trout in the river.

But not with that fly. I must have shown it to fifty trout but I never had another taker. I've kept the nymph in my box ever since as a reminder of

my youthful presumptions. Over the years I have
shown it to trout in many places, and not one has
given it more than a glance. It was quite a while
before I discovered its fault—it tried to be a
too-perfect imitation.

This might sound like a paradox, but I have
seldom had much luck with nymphs that attempt
to imitate the real thing down to the last body
segment and leg. But a nymph that is shaggily
suggestive—ah!

I wasn't to tumble to this right away. One day I
asked a nymph fisherman I'd seen at Titicus time
and again catching fish, what he used.

"Beat-up old Hare's Ear or March Brown in a
No. 10 for this creek," he said. "Here. Try one of
mine; I'm through anyway." He bit off the March

After I learned where all the
fish in Titicus Outlet lived, it
was then easy to catch them
on wet flies or nymphs in the
early season.

Brown he was using and handed it to me.

It was frazzled, all right. So much, in fact, that I wondered if it might have passed its usefulness. The fly had caught so many fish it was in a stage somewhere between being a wet fly and a nymph.

The fisherman must have noticed my doubting look. "Fish can't tell what it is, so they take it," he said, and left the stream.

I didn't catch trout with that fly until I remembered how the fish had taken natural baits. Almost invariably a trout would dart from its station and take the bait while executing a turn. Then back it went. This quick turn gave me a flashing glimpse of the trout's side. Often I couldn't feel a trout the moment it took a live bait, but a lot of the time I could tell by its action what had happened.

Watching for this flash near the nymph (sometimes there'd be just a swirl) helped me hook my first trout on the worn old March Brown. Later I made some flies that were deliberately ragged, along with some Gold-Rib Hare's Ears, and these two flies, which were actually nymphs in the condition that they were in, were all I used for years on Titicus.

Some common baits to be found in or near a stream: from left, salamander; from top, caddis-fly case (there's a pale-yellow nymph inside), hellgrammite, and leech.

The technique had to be different in the slow water of upper pools, however. There was less need for a trout to hurry because there wasn't a fast current to sweep a morsel from its reach if it didn't lunge swiftly. The quiet-pool trout would coast up to a nymph and, unless a fish followed almost to the bank, in which case the trout made a swirling strike, the fish would merely spurt forward a little and engulf the nymph. There would be no flash, no swirl. But there would be a momentary white blob where the nymph had been—the whiteness of the trout's open mouth as it took. If the water is clear you'd be surprised how far away you can see this.

A couple of years ago, I found a nymph to fish as a hellgrammite on Titicus. I was comparing fly boxes with Ted Trueblood at the start of a trip, and he gave me a big nymph I'd admired—a creation an inch or so long, all brown chenille in the body with a humped thorax that was yellow underneath. A twist or two of sparse hackle up front suggested legs, and a pair of goose-quill fibers suggested the pronged tail.

"It's a Madison River Stone Fly," Ted explained. "We grow 'em big out West."

I thought to myself that Titicus trout would think it was a hellgrammite—and they did just that. The point is that here was a nymph that could be mistaken for another underwater species because it happened to be about the right shape and color. That's why the nymphed March Brown and Hare's Ear worked in Titicus. They were about the shape, size, and color of local nymphs.

I now get along in most places with just four nymph patterns: a gray, brown, and tan, all with shaggy hair bodies, and the big stone-fly pattern. When I go to a strange river and no fish are showing, I'm apt to toss a hookless Colorado around to see what flashes at it, then I turn over rocks to find out the size and color of the nymphs. One of my four nymphs usually catches some of the trout that reveal themselves to my Colorado.

Thanks to watching trout and studying the water of my pet small stream, I don't find it difficult to guess where the trout will be lying in bigger rivers. I look for the slow spots near a main current, and instead of tossing in bark chips nowadays to see how food will be carried to waiting trout, I watch the bubbles on the surface.

Ever since that first day with Polaroid glasses at the Titicus meadow pool when I stepped forward and spooked a trout that had been lying almost at my feet, I approach even the biggest river with extreme care. This brings me to a great, untapped source of trout ignored by many—bankside fish.

When land insects such as grasshoppers, crickets, ants, sowbugs, and caterpillars fall into a stream, they generally do it near a bank, or close enough so they are swept along the bank. In the hot summer, when the bank grasses are long, trout love to lurk underneath, near cover, shade, and an eventual morsel.

The way to locate these fish swiftly is to float a live, kicking insect to them. I did this on Titicus mostly with grasshoppers, since there were lots of them. But I soon learned that you can't just toss a hopper in and wait for results—the critter will sink. You must place the hopper on the surface carefully so that it won't break through the film. Send it on its way no more than six inches from the bank. Pick a straight stretch for the longest possible float, then hold your breath.

While trying this out one day, I lay on my stomach and plucked out one of the grasshoppers I'd stuffed into a compartment of my dry-fly box. The first one caught at a bit of trailing grass only a yard below me and crawled out. But the second sailed kicking along the bank for ten feet before disappearing in a smother of foam.

A trout there? I'd never have guessed.

After giving the trout a few minutes to swallow the hopper, I sent another down the bank, but with a small hook in it. On and on it sailed. It reached the target zone. Nothing. I let out my breath. But a little farther on the trout came for it like a tiger. It was a jewel of a fourteen-inch brook trout.

Here was a trout that had probably known a lifetime of seclusion. How many times it must have been alerted by careless treading on the bank and by anglers wading unknowing (as I had all summer) past its doorstep.

In those days I didn't have the excellent Joe's Hopper and other patterns that imitate the grasshopper. I didn't have silicone dressing that dries on the fly and leaves no telltale oil rings on the surface. I didn't have ultrafine monofilament that is double the strength of what was then the finest gut. But one thing has not changed—the need for developing good technique.

While I'm on the subject of trout downtrodden by the rush of eager novices to the river, let me tell you one last bit about bankside fishing. It's only a matter of six inches, but not knowing about it years ago must have cost me scores of trout.

You can catch some trout by dropping your fly half-a-foot from the bank. You can also interest most of the trout—and catch more, bigger warier fish—if the fly just brushes past the grass trailing in the water.

It's the combination of a lot of little things that make a trout fisherman, not just a caster. I think you learn them quickest and best on a small stream. It's like fishing through a picture window.

How to Beat Trout

That Spurn Dry Flies

IT'S STRANGE HOW you can live with something of importance you have learned and not put it to good use immediately. I hit upon a good trout-fishing idea many years ago, but only cashed in on it later. Recently the trouble was that what I had learned was in such contradiction to what I'd come to believe, that my discovery seemed a mistake.

If you fish a dry fly you may have thought, as I did, that when trout are rising freely it's a waste of time to use anything else.

Well, it isn't necessarily so.

You can catch them on a worm, a spinner, a wet fly, a——. But let me begin at the beginning. One evening on the West Branch of the Croton River, which is in Putnam County, New York, and is fished hard all season long, I came upon rising trout in the big first pool—the one that existed before the present concrete bridge for the new road was built. The trout were only a car's length from the bank. It was dusk, and I had a small worm on a small hook, for I'd been fishing a spring hole downstream.

Just on impulse, I cast the worm as delicately as

I could above the trout and, holding the rod erect for better feel, I let the worm drift toward the fish. Twice I hauled in slack and raised the tip gently to keep the worm near the surface. A brown trout about a foot long took, and I caught him.

There still was a little worm left. I caught another brownie with it, but he jumped so much he put the others down, and I quit after landing him. That was 25 years ago.

I put the whole thing down as a freak experience, and didn't even try it again for three or four years. Then one afternoon on the East Branch of the Ausable, in upper New York, where I was spending a summer vacation, the trout began to rise. I went after them with dry flies, but I couldn't catch any. Since they continued to feed, I went ashore and began to turn over rocks looking for a worm. I found one, and presently landed a worthwhile brown trout. Then I put down four in a row and was about to abandon the idea when I caught another, my last.

From this and other experiences I've come to believe that the worm should be quite small so it won't sink quickly, and fixed on the lightest of fly-tying hooks. The drift should be short, say ten feet at most, and it helps if most of the leader is dry enough to float (the worm will always sink the last foot or so). Finally, the worm must drift naturally.

I've had best luck when I could conceal the splash of the worm landing in the water. One way to do this is to cast onto a rock, then pluck the worm into the current. Another is to cast behind an object—a bush or a rock—upstream of the trout, then draw the bait into the current before its drift begins.

I've only caught brown trout with this method, but that's probably because they happened to be the abundant species in the streams I've fished. They're hard to fool with flies, however, and I don't see why the system wouldn't work with other, not so finicky trout.

Now here is an odd thing. I'd proved to myself that rising trout could be taken with worms as a second method to dry flies, yet it didn't occur to me to try a third. And since I'd rather fish a fly than anything else, I put the worm business on the back shelf, so to speak, for use only in case of emergency.

The discovery of the third way came about through curiosity. One June day I came upon several rising fish on a stretch of the Ten Mile River in lower Connecticut. It was almost noon and the water was fairly clear. I tried several dry flies without luck, and finally began to wonder whether the rising fish were trout. The Ten Mile also has a large population of chubs, plus some bass and sunfish.

So I tried to find out what the rising fish were, and put on a 4/0 brass Colorado spinner. I'd often seen trout flash out of feeding position to examine a passing Colorado, and it occurred to me I might provoke a fish or two into revealing themselves.

I cast upstream of the first riser and worked the spinner so it crossed near the fish. The fish flashed briefly as the Colorado passed, and the motion was so quick I thought it might be a trout. After a while, I tried again and this time the fish nailed the spinner hard. It was a plump little rainbow, and its stomach was crammed with small dark flies. A little later I caught another which had been feeding to one side of the others.

Since then I've tried a Colorado on rising trout several times, and I've found it works equally well on brooks, browns, and rainbows. And once on the Big Lost River in Idaho, fishing with Sun Valley guides Taylor Williams and Don Anderson, I came upon a rising fish that spurned our flies but hit a small Colorado. It was a 2-pound whitefish.

There are certain things to know if you're to

succeed with a Colorado among rising trout. Bright light seems to be a necessity. Unless the sun is actually shining on the water, I've found it a waste of time to try the method, either in early morning or during an evening rise.

Color and size of the spinner also are important. Brass seems far and away best to me, but not shiny brass—I always dull a new Colorado by rubbing its blade with earth. Brass on one side of the blade and nickel on the other is a combination I sometimes have luck with, if the water is a little roiled. The all-nickel has been so poor I've given it up. The slower you fish a Colorado among rising trout, the better, and this practically dictates the size. The tiny 4/0 has such a small blade it must be worked very fast for best results. The slightly larger 3/0 seems superior.

I think the deadliest way to use this spinner is on a nine-foot leader tapered to 3X. A longer leader is hard to make turn over at the end of a cast, and one tapered to a finer point just doesn't seem to work as well. If possible, try to make an upstream cast to one side of a feeding trout— almost straight upstream. You have to hold the rod fairly high and strip line quickly to keep the spinner turning and floating. Actually, the spinner must be pulled downstream a little.

Then, as the flashing fraud draws near the trout, look out. Often the fish will wallop it head on. Sometimes one will dart downstream after it and strike two or three times in quick succession.

The more conventional way to fish the Colorado is slightly upstream and across, letting the current belly the floating line so there's always enough pressure to keep the spinner rotating. Once, when a friend was trying out this business, I climbed a tree that overhung the stream and watched the proceedings with Polaroid glasses.

There were several trout in a group; perhaps a dozen. At the first pass of the Colorado, most of them stirred nervously, and one detached itself and sped after the spinner as it passed. But he missed, and immediately returned to his former station. On the second cast, the trout again seemed edgy, and the next time two trout made for the spinner and one took solidly. After considerable resting of the pool, John McLain, my fishing partner, tried again, but the fish didn't react at all, and the few more casts he made only put them down.

The most baffling time for dry-fly men is when streams get low and the trout feed on midges— those tiny little flies that fuss around rocks out in the middle of the creek. You can't make them out well enough to try to match them. One day I learned that midging trout can be caught on a tiny wet fly.

What makes the occasion stick in my memory is because of what happened to Ed Lyon, who was fishing with me on the New York end of the Ten Mile. He'd tried his last small dry-fly pattern, and when the trout spurned it, he gave a mighty yank of resentment. The fly flew out and stuck in his upper lip. That put him out of action for a time. He didn't want to do anything but sit in the car and worry the fly loose, so I kept on, finally trying a very sparsely dressed wet fly on a No. 16 hook.

A trout took it so casually it almost seemed a mistake. I'd made a long cast, given the line a twitch to jerk under the end of the leader, and a little later moved the fly a few inches, paused, and was repeating when the strike came.

I yelled, Ed gave his lipped fly a last desperate pull that freed it, and I landed a bouncy 12-inch brown trout. We didn't drain the pool of fish, catching only three more between us, but we felt each trout caught under these conditions was a triumph.

From season to season this method has worked when nothing else I tried would interest trout, but it wasn't until recently that I found out why.

Apparently when the developing midge passes from the larval to the pupal stage, it rises to the top in slow water where its hairlike respiratory apparatus breaks through the surface film. The pupa then dangles vertically under the film. Any disturbance sends it diving down, though it soon returns to the surface.

Trout feed on these pupa and on the mature flies indiscriminately. It's easy to see how working a little wet fly near the surface in these circumstances will take trout. Light-colored patterns have given me best results.

The worm works best in the shade or in poor light, the Colorado is a sunshine lure, and the tiny wet fly is a low-water specialty. But what I've found out about streamers and dry-fly-minded trout seems to work any time or day.

I'm not talking about springtime, of course, for everyone knows how effective streamers are then. Summertime periods are what I have in mind.

When Ted Trueblood lived in the East before World War II, he, Dan Holland and I used to work the rivers in New York's Westchester and Putnam Counties. One Sunday afternoon we stopped by the upper end of the West Branch of the Croton River. It was August and a time of clear, fairly low water, and we'd been fishing for bass with fly rods and streamer flies.

We looked down from the road bridge and saw a fair-size brown trout lying in a current a few inches below the surface.

"We'll never catch him," I said.

Dan agreed. This pool by the road undoubtedly had taken a hard beating over the weekend.

"I'm not so sure," Ted remarked.

He casually began to work out line, and presently cast a bass bucktail well upstream of the trout. When the fly was only a few feet above the fish, Ted yanked his line a couple of times to make

Dry-fly fishing for trout. The angler kneels in an attempt at partial concealment for fish in this clear water in lower New York state.

the fly dart, and the trout all but swallowed it in its eagerness.

I put the affair down as a freak. We fished the stream a while with dry flies, caught nothing more, and went on to some other place. Then one Saturday Dan Holland and I looked down from the high bank of a rather low Westchester stream, and happened to see a big brown trout come out from under a rock. The rock was the only cover in a pool that was perhaps thirty feet long and half as wide. The trout cruised the pool unhurriedly, and took two flies off the surface before it went back under the rock.

We decided that I'd fish the pool with a wet fly while Dan directed the show from above. The water was so clear and calm we figured it would be impossible to get results with a dry fly, so our plan was for me to make a cast when the trout was under the rock, sink the line and leader, and start to move the fly when the trout circled the pool again.

Fearing the trout might not notice a wet fly unless he was right on top of it, I put on a small streamer.

"O.K.," said Dan. "Cast."

I cast to the far side, jerked the line and leader under, and waited. About ten minutes later Dan began to get excited.

"He's out and headed your way," he said, peering down.

The trout took a natural off the surface, and my heart jumped when I saw its snout break the surface.

"He's still coming. You'd better move the fly right now."

I plucked in half a foot of line, and saw a heavy wake rushing toward my streamer. I gave the line another twitch and felt the trout. What a commotion in that shallow pool! The fish was 19 inches long, and he leaped like a young tarpon.

To these incidents a third was later added on the Schoharie, which is in New York's Catskill Mountains area. Fly fishing was slow, with few rising trout. Then I saw a bunch of little bass rise. From experience I knew that bass are hard to hook on a small dry fly, so I put on a streamer.

They were small and dumb, and I worked my way through, catching and releasing them. Then one of the "bass" turned out to be a decent-sized rainbow. Before I'd either put down or caught the others, I hooked another rainbow that was the twin of the first.

It seemed like one of those screwy things which at the time doesn't appear particularly pertinent, and it didn't occur to me to link it to the two

Don't go dry-fly fishing without baby streamers and bucktails. This rainbow was caught on a small bucktail.

other times when trout had taken a streamer under dry-fly conditions.

But I never quite forgot the incident, and after the war I was glad I hadn't. Walking the shallows of a quiet pool one day, I scared a minnow which had lurked unseen until I got close. It shot away, leaving a little muddy cloud behind, and it struck me that this was what had happened the time I yanked my streamer into life as Dan Holland directed operations from above. A puff of mud or silt in the water, I reasoned, would alert a trout that a minnow (or streamer) was near by.

I've put this to good use three times since then, when conditions were right—the shallow pool, the rising trout, the trap set with a sunken streamer. But it's hardly a substitute for ordinary dry-fly fishing.

Then, a few summers ago, I found out what I'd had clues to all along. This time the theory didn't come first; I had to make a mistake by putting fly boxes in my pockets.

I'd gone to the Shepaug, a lovely winding stream in western Connecticut, and found trout rising to a small, whitish May fly. The first box I pulled out contained my dark dry flies, and I'd made a mistake with the other—instead of containing light-colored drys, it held big wets and small streamers.

Rather than go back to the car for the other box, I decided to try a streamer. It had finally percolated through to me that when trout are rising they're hungry, and you don't always have to give them dry flies. I put on a miniature Gray Ghost, 1¼ inches long, and cast above the fish. When I knew it was among them, I began to jolt it by yanking the line. A fat rainbow took it immediately. So help me, every time that fly got in among the rising trout and I began to work it in little short spurts, there was action of some kind. It seemed to excite them. A couple of times trout actually jumped over the streamer.

The limit at that time was six trout, and I took it in less than an hour. A couple of weeks later I did it again, though not so quickly. Since then I've repeated the performance enough times to become convinced I'd be foolish to go dry-fly fishing without taking along my miniature streamers and baby bucktails. My notion is that when a streamer drifting along just below the surface suddenly comes to life amid a bunch of surfacing trout, it's taken for a stunned minnow with just enough energy left to panic at the sight of its traditional enemy.

This method has fooled brook, brown, and rainbow trout. It seems most effective if the current is a little bumpy; perhaps this conceals traces of the leader being jerked, such as bubbles at the knots. My best luck has been with dark patterns tied on a hook not more than an inch long. Larger, heavier flies seem to sink too readily, and they can't be worked properly.

I don't propose these ideas out of dissatisfaction with dry-fly fishing—I really enjoy it. But it also can be frustrating, especially when others have worked over the pools before you and helped to wise up the fish. Next time it looks as if you're going to take a dry-fly licking, try something unconventional. You may chance upon even more revolutionary ways than mine for saving the day.

Western Flies for

Early Eastern Trout

AS WE DROVE north through lower Connecticut one recent May day to fish the Shepaug, a lovely meandering trout stream of rocky pools shaded by hemlocks and sugar maples, my guest Jim Rikhoff asked the eternal question:

"What do you think they'll take?"

I just about *knew* what was going to work, but I was evasive. I had never cast a fly with Jim, who works for the Winchester-Western Division of Olin Corp., so I had no clues to his ability. And you know how it is when you want to show an old friend good fishing—too often it's poor.

So all I said was, "You're in for a surprise."

A short time later we were standing beside the first pool. The Shepaug was up a little and fairly clear—a typical spring situation on trout streams in the East. Concealing a smile, I handed Jim a rather large wet fly.

"What the devil's *that*?" he asked.

Clearly, he thought I was putting him on.

"Steelhead fly," I said. "A good trout finder. They'll flash at it even if they don't take, and then if you want to switch to something else, you'll know exactly where the trout are."

Giving me a hard stare, Rikhoff tied on the fly and moved up the bank toward the head of the pool. I knotted on a fly of the same pattern and began casting about fifty yards downstream from my friend.

Peeking through a cloud of pipe smoke, I noticed that Jim's casting was okay. Even better, he was working the fly properly. Now it was up to the brookies, rainbows, and browns that I knew had recently been stocked; for the Shepaug, like most Connecticut streams, needs a generous replenishing of its trout every springtime.

In about ten minutes I heard a mighty yell. Jim had a trout on, and as I watched, it leaped a yard into the sparkling May sunlight. Three times the fish vaulted clear as I hurried along the bank.

This brown trout from the Shepaug fell victim to Thor, one of the weighted steelhead patterns shown in flybox.

"Must be foul-hooked," I remarked meanly. "Our trout don't usually jump like that."

"Foul-hooked my grandmother!" Jim said.

Presently he netted a 14-inch rainbow, hooked fair in the jaw. Then he rinsed the fly and gazed thoughtfully at it—fat red chenille body, red tail, polar-bear wings, a wisp of dark-brown hackles at the throat, No. 4 hook.

"It's a weighted Thor," I told him. "A steelhead fly, as I mentioned. Not quite a streamer. Works best if you let it sink for a few seconds, then retrieve with short pulls so it struggles along the bottom of the pool."

We separated and resumed fishing. Soon I caught a brookie, 10 inches or so, after which the pool seemed to go dead. We moved along to the next pool. On Jim's first cast a trout splashed at his fly as he lifted it from the water, and I heard the breath go out of him in disappointment.

How I came to use weighted Western flies on Eastern trout was accidental. In May of 1960 I was passing through Anchorage, Alaska, en route to a hunt for brown bears on the Alaska Peninsula. I had heard there would be some river fishing for rainbows, so I rented some tackle and bought flies from the late Harry L. Swank Jr.'s store in Anchorage.

"Don't get anything but these weighted steelhead flies," Harry advised me. "The water is big and deep, and the trout will be right on the bottom."

He was right but only the dark patterns worked. So I came home with a dozen weighted Thors and other bright steelhead wet flies in a new aluminum clip box.

Not one of these flies was used until the following spring when my wife, who is not an accomplished angler, snapped off a fly I had given her. She didn't want to risk losing another of my

home-tied favorites, so she put on a Thor and hurled it across the Shepaug. Then in the way of happy coincidences, she unthinkingly let the fly sink deep while she lit a cigarette. She'd hardly begun to retrieve the fly when she hooked a hefty trout. That was the beginning.

At the time I didn't place much significance on this event, and Pris and I both laughed about her "Mother's Day trout." I had been fishing the Shepaug regularly for six years, and though the river has plenty of minnows, I'd had only spotty results with minnow-imitating flies such as the Gray Ghost streamer and the Brown-and-White bucktail. Most of my spring luck had been with small wet flies and nymphs.

"Hang in there, Jim," I said. "You got 'em all stirred up."

Rikhoff now had a fine bead of sweat on his brow. For the third time, a trout had swirled behind his fly without taking.

Suddenly he sat down.

"I'm going to give them a rest," he said.

Jim got out a cigarette—something he usually reserves for trying situations—and inhaled.

"I can see the trout follow the fly up, and then I get paralyzed," he complained.

"Try a little deeper and slower," I suggested as Jim shook out line for another shot at the trout a little later.

I was standing above him on a rock ledge and watching the water with Polaroid glasses. Jim cast straight upstream, and I could just make out the Thor drifting near the bottom in the current at the head of the pool.

Just then Jim lifted his rod, and as the fly began to ascend, a shadowy form detached itself from the

n Rikhoff admires 2-pound
nbow that hit a Thor.

Because he was working the fly too fast, Jim missed trout here three tim camouflage of the bottom and drifted upward with the fly. The trout, a good-sized brookie, followed the fly almost to the surface before turning away.

Rikhoff looked around, glassy-eyed.

"What did I do wrong?" he asked.

"You forgot to twitch the fly."

Well-programmed now, Jim presently caught a rainbow as I wandered downstream to fish a deep spot that usually held some trout.

Half an hour later we broke for lunch, and I could tell that my friend no longer thought the weighted Thor was ridiculous. It is hard to argue against as respectable a catch as we had spread out in the shade to admire while we ate our lunch beside the river.

"Every time I throw that thing in the water," Jim remarked, "I can't believe it is going to work. It looks downright improper."

"Granted," I said.

"We're in the hard-fished East, man," Jim continued. "You *know* that the most successful way to catch trout here is with good imitations—nymphs and wet flies such as the March Brown early, then dry flies later."

I took a side road to make a point.

"Would you fish this fly in Maine for trout after ice-out?" I asked.

"Sure. It would be great. It's practically a Royal Coachman."

"And how would you describe Maine trout in the early spring?"

"Hungry and eager and sort of dumb," Jim said.

I pointed out that these Shepaug trout had left the hatchery only about ten days ago. I mentioned that two trout I'd caught and gutted that morning had no insect life in their stomachs, though one had eaten a small minnow.

"I don't think these fish know what a nymph is yet," I said. "But they *are* hungry, eager and dumb."

Rikhoff nodded grudgingly.

Between sandwiches, I told Jim how I first made a killing with a Thor on the Shepaug. It was the spring after Pris's Mother's Day trout, and the river was somewhat muddy and a bit high. After trying various flies, I put on a Thor pretty much in desperation and because I knew it would go deep. That day I took a limit of five trout and released several more.

"I thought my success was in some way accidental," I remarked, "that maybe the trout could only make out a big bright fly in that cloudy water."

But the next weekend the Shepaug was lower and clear. Out of curiosity I tried a Thor first, and once again the trout attacked it in force. That was the breakthrough. I finally realized I was doing something right, but I wasn't quite sure what it was.

I had several patterns of weighted steelhead flies that were tied on No. 4 and No. 6 hooks, and I tried many of them carefully. I soon found that patterns with a lot of hot orange or red were hopeless. And predominantly pale-gray flies such as the Burlap or Gray Hackle hardly brought a follow. To my surprise all-dark flies such as the handsome Black Prince were quite poor. One dark pattern with a white-tipped wing of silver squirrel hair—the Atomic—proved fair on the rare days when the trout wouldn't take a Thor or the similar Hairwing Royal Coachman or other mostly-white patterns with red on their bodies such as the Umpqua Special.

Jim has his hands full with a cartwheeling rainbow on Shepaug.

"What about weighted nymphs?" Jim asked.

"Poor this early," I said, "and later you don't need them weighted."

Presently we separated to fish the next two pools, and it wasn't long before I heard a faint but exultant cry echo through the woods—"It still works!"

At this point you may well wonder—okay, but will weighted steelhead flies work on other recently stocked streams?

Two steelhead flies that are spring killers in the East: Atomic, left, and Thor.

I pondered this question myself and resolved to find out. So the next April and early May I fished two streams I know well in lower New York's Westchester County—Titicus Outlet and Amawalk Outlet. Farther north, in Dutchess County, I tried the Ten Mile River. Results were encouraging, and I learned something besides.

First I fished Titicus, described earlier. I soon found that in most of its fairly shallow water I couldn't fish a weighted Thor at all because it kept hanging up on the rocky bottom. Two pools were about a yard deep but were rather confined, making it difficult to work the fly well and remain concealed from the trout. I had no luck.

As a result of this experience, I decided that broad shallow streams would be hopeless. To keep the fly off the bottom in such waters you must fish it too fast.

Next I tried Amawalk Outlet, another oversize brook. Amawalk, however, has more different types of water than Titicus and is restricted to fly fishing only. The daily limit is one fish, and the fish must be at least 14 inches long. Early in the season the Amawalk is heavily stocked, and I decided that it would be ideal test water.

Once again I flunked in the shallow pools because I had to work the fly too fast. I could see trout in some of these pools, but they showed no interest in the fly.

I then moved to a deep pool about 25 feet square where the stream hurls itself over an old colonial wall and cascades perhaps twelve feet. The spray from the falls beads the angler who approaches from below. It's a real beauty spot, and once, years ago, I caught a 21-inch brown here on a streamer.

In half an hour I caught three 10- to 12-inch trout on a Thor, and of course I had to release them all. Farther downstream, at a deep bend pool, another 10-incher hit on the second or third tug as I raised the fly off the bottom.

By now it was midmorning and fishermen were so numerous that there was no more undisturbed water. I left, convinced that success with these weighted flies depended on using them in deep pools or slow stretches of big water, a description that fits the Shepaug perfectly.

Finally, on a cold miserable day, I tried the Ten Mile, which was so crowded with anglers that I just about had to stand in line, a common condition in the East for the first few weeks of the season. Eventually a bait fisherman quit a rock that offered a good position for making long casts both across the river and downstream, and I took the spot.

On the first cast I got a heavy strike and my heart lifted. There are big wild trout in the Ten Mile along with the recently stocked fish. But this fish was weak and proved to be a large chub. I caught two more chubs and then a little small-mouth bass. At last a 9-inch brookie took hold.

Material for tying a weighted Thor.

The steps in tying, top to bottom from right: 1. Wax tying thread and attach to shank of No. 4 or No. 6 standard wet-fly hook, ribbing shank and finishing with a half-hitch above the hook bend; tie on tail, using fibers from red or orange hackle feather, tie on 020-inch-diameter lead wire where shoulder of fly will be, wrap it back to base of tail, and secure with thread, leaving wire dangling from its spool. 2. Lay red chenille along top of hook and secure it by wrapping thread lightly toward front of hook and tying off at head position. 3. Now wrap lead wire closely from tail to shoulder; tie off. 4. Overwrap lead with chenille and tie off at shoulder. 5. Hold hair (white bucktail, impala, or polar bear) against top of hook and attach with firm wraps of thread and a half-hitch; trim excess hair in front. 6. Tie in brown hackle fibers at throat, finish wrapping head, and finally apply fly cement.

Twenty minutes later I caught its twin and quit—frozen but sure now that our experiences on the Shepaug hadn't been some sort of wild mistake.

Working a weighted steelhead fly along the bottom is not difficult. Mostly you just cast the fly across a run or pool, a few yards upstream of the area you want to cover. Then you twitch the fly across the bottom. A dead drift is seldom effective.

Toward the end of your cross-stream retrieve—or after a quartering-downstream or straight-down-stream cast—the fly is best retrieved by stripping in line with short, quick jerks. In deep water it is often effective to strip the fly rather steeply toward the surface and then let it fall back to the depths again at intervals during your bottom retrieve.

Rikhoff nets a 2-pound rainbow; one of the fish that prompted him to say this was the best spring fishing.

But suppose you want to work deep water with a good current directly opposite you? Jim Rikhoff and I were now looking at such a stretch. A strong, slick current swept past a rocky outcrop at the head of a pool some 200 yards long.

"Often the best trout in the pool," I said, "are lying at the bottom of that current, six feet down, for first crack at any food that sweeps past."

Jim looked at me suspiciously.

"You've put me in a mean place, buster," he said.

"Nope. This is the best spot in the river. But the fly *must* move downstream in little spurts along the bottom."

"It's impossible," Jim said. "We're right beside the fish, and they'll see me."

So I told him about a technique used in British Columbia to swim a fly downstream faster than the current in imitation of sockeye-salmon fry on the move. Jim made a 25-foot cast upstream, then quickly turned and lowered his rod tip and pointed it downstream.

"Wait," I cautioned.

Quickly the current made a U in his line at the surface.

"Now start stripping," I said. "Keep the rod pointed downstream."

By pulling line against the current on his side of the U, Jim was hurrying the sinking fly downstream on the other side of the U.

"I think you're putting me on," he said, still working hard.

"No, you're doing it just right. The fly should be passing you about now."

On the third time through, Jim tied into a lusty rainbow that shot up barely a yard away and showered us with spray.

"It's too deep for them to see you," I said.

Jim was too busy with the fish to hear me.

"All you have to do is keep that fly moving near the bottom," I continued.

The trout leaped again.

"I don't think they know just what the fly is," I went on, "but it is down where they are, and when it moves one often grabs it."

Jim wasn't listening. The rainbow uncorked a stiff run down the current, and Rikhoff was happy and sort of crooning to the fish. He eventually landed it—about a two-pounder, the best fish of the day.

Now we walked down a woods path toward more fishing. Jim asked if a fly fisherman could not get the same effect by sinking an ordinary fly with split shot on the leader ahead of it or by using a fine lead-wire wrap on the leader. I told him that when my original supply of Alaskan Thors began to run out I tried this very thing and didn't like the results. A shot too often got hung up on the bottom. And whether I used a shot or a wire wrap, I thought the fly tended to flutter and flop about unnaturally in currents.

So I turned to tying my own and found that a lead-core No. 4 or 6 fly weighing 11 to 12 grains was just about right. This weight is two to three times as great as that of an unweighted fly of the same size. I also found that a slow-sinking line worked best with these flies in the Eastern waters I've tried so far. I get by with my regular 8-foot trout rod, since I don't usually have to make long casts. If I do, the light rod and heavy fly would not make a very efficient combination. And I've learned to duck my head when I make a sloppy backcast with one of these flies.

At length we came to the last pool, where the current piled itself against a rock bank and turned abruptly left. This was my fourteenth year of fishing on the Shepaug, and I knew that the likeliest area for catching a trout in this pool was near the tail, where the bottom shelved up from eight or ten feet deep to about three.

"In this pool," I said to Jim, "you have to let the current take the fly and then carry it several yards to the left."

I don't think he quite believed me.

"How can you hook a trout when your line has a ninety-degree bend in it?" he asked.

"Just yank hard," I said.

I yanked hard about ten minutes later and caught a dandy brown as a result. Then we hiked back to the car. Jim was somewhat ecstatic.

"How long does all this last?" he wanted to know.

"Till the water warms up and the trout start feeding on insects," I said. "If it's a cool spring, I fish the Thor through May."

"And after that?"

"Forget it."

"You mean, this is strictly a cold-water fly for dumb hatchery trout?"

"Exactly," I said.

Presently we were back at the car and taking down our tackle. Covertly I watched Rikhoff bite off his Thor and set it aside. He made some remark about the day's having produced the greatest spring fishing he'd had in years, even though he still couldn't quite believe it.

"I'll make you a present of that fly," I said, in what by now had become a ritual with my spring fishing companions on the Shepaug.

"Good," he said. "I was going to keep it anyway."

Old Friends and

the Joys of the Worm

IT WAS JOHN McLain's turn at the rod. He lifted it, got the worm swinging well and then carefully lobbed it to the head of the next pool. As the current swept the worm along, McLain lowered the rod so the line would flow easily through the guides.

Ed Lyon and I watched. We were sprawled on a bank of the stream, drinking beer and smoking. The May sun warmed us and scented the air with the fragrance of fallen spruce needles. Somewhere downstream a ruffed grouse drummed because it was a lovely spring day.

It had been about twenty years since the three of us fished this brook in the Catskill Mountains of New York, and little had changed up here on the lonely Roaring Kill. Or to the old house overlooking it. McLain, Lyon, and other school friends in their Goose and Gander Club had scraped together $500 in the middle thirties to buy the long-empty house and acreage. We had all become graduate worm fishermen on the Kill, which ran only twenty yards from the back door.

"The back porch looks good," I remarked to Ed. "Must have been patched up."

Some pretty good beer parties used to get thrown here. As a consequence, beer, soup, coffee and whatnot got spilled on the weathered wood of the back porch. This proved to be a strong attraction for porcupines and they practically ate the porch out from under us in a few years. But now it had been fixed.

"We have a big woodchuck living under the front porch. Maybe he keeps the porcupines away," Ed told me.

One seldom sees a brookie longer than 9 or 10 inches from the Roaring Kill. These fish, 6 to 8 inches long, are mature and will spawn in the fall.

Just then McLain gave a yell and whipped his worm into some overhead branches. This was always a problem up here near the Notch—the brook is so overgrown with trees that you just about *have* to fish a worm. We were doing this out of choice, however, because it had long been the

custom. I'd even bought a wicker creel for the occasion, which McLain was now wearing as sloppily as when he was a school kid.

"Big one!" he shouted at us over the splashing of the brook.

"Did you ever sell the picture of the porcupine drinking gin to Seagram's?" Ed asked, as if it had been last weekend.

On arriving at the house, the first chore used to be chasing off the porcupines with a pole or a board. Sometimes a reluctant porcupine got killed. One morning we had a dead porky which I propped up against the back steps. It looked quite lifelike. Then I happened to see an empty bottle of Seagram's King Arthur gin. I put some water in the bottle and into a shot glass and set them handy to

John McLain fishing the Kill a little below the house.

the porcupine. Then someone put a lit cigarette into a corner of the porcupine's mouth and after the ash had lengthened, I took a memorable color picture. Full of anticipation, I sent the transparency to the ad agency handling Seagram's but I guess they felt that a porcupine wasn't much of a recommendation for the brand. I got the picture back.

At this point John McLain derricked a fish from the Roaring Kill. We crowded close to admire the first catch—a brook trout about 8-inches long and vibrantly colored. "He was as fussy as a salmon," McLain declared. "I had forgotten how carefully you have to let the worm float freely."

Ed Lyon now took up the rod, creel and bait box.

I fished a beer from the Kill and handed it icy-cold to McLain. We lit our pipes and lay back, half-watching Ed.

"Remember the first meal I cooked on the old stove?" John was recalling a startling occasion. He, Ed and I had driven north to the old house shortly after it was first bought. It was late in the fall and a drift of snow lay across the kitchen floor. It had fallen in through a hole in the shed roof above. We were so famished we decided to have a meal immediately and forget about the snow.

We stuffed the cast-iron range full of wood which happened to be somewhat damp. The fire wouldn't catch so John poured a liberal dose of kerosene on the wood and replaced the stove lid. Nothing happened. We were sitting in three rickety chairs facing the stove, waiting for warmth.

"You were pretty mean with that kerosene," Ed Lyon remarked.

McLain removed two stove lids this time and

This is the dead porcupine I photographed on the back steps of the house. I sent a copy of the picture in color the ad agency handling Seagrams but the agency didn't consider this a good enough endorsement. They discontinued the brand not long afterward.

really sloshed kerosene around. Meanwhile, a tiny flame was working up through the kindling.

Suddenly there was a roar and the heavy iron lids flew upward, turning lazily end over end like tossed pancakes. We fell over backwards onto the snow. The fire had started at last.

"What did we do about the snow?"

"We let it melt and then mopped it out the back door."

Ed Lyon looked around at us with a wide grin.

"He's got one on," John said. "I never saw a more thorough worm fisherman."

Presently Ed flicked the rod to set the hook and drew a small trout splashing from the Kill. "He's too small," Ed said. The trout was only about 5-inches long.

Ed Lyon fishing a pool of the Roaring Kill.

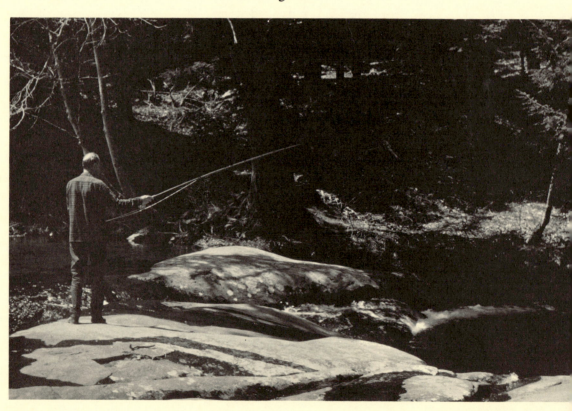

"There is no minimum length in New York any more," I remarked. "Let's keep it for breakfast."

I took the rod and paraphernalia, reflecting that I still had some Thomas rods and a Garrison with black dots applied with India ink, then varnished over, exactly six inches apart. Later, when the New York minimum went to seven inches, I added a bar with the number 7 above it. Perhaps it was the effect of the Great Depression, but every keepable trout got kept when I was a youngster, and usually was listed by exact measurement in a journal besides.

I threaded on a worm, starting at the head—how long ago *that* had been!—and swung the bait toward a dark swirly bit of water at the beginning of the next hole.

If my fly-casting friends could only see me now, I thought with a grin, and lifted the rod gently to check for the throb of a trout worrying the worm.

Suddenly, I recalled an anguished moment of my youth at a deep pool on the West Branch of the Croton River in southern New York. The night-crawler I was using washed unexpectedly to the surface and I raised the rod sharply in annoyance to make a fresh cast. Just as the worm left the water a brook trout of astonishing length and depth made a pass at the worm and missed.

Then I remembered standing beside a tiny brook in the Adirondacks and idly dunking a worm in a pool with an overhung, grassy bank at my feet. The brookie that swept out, engulfed the worm, and disappeared was a foot long—a giant for that rivulet. I can still recall the spooky feeling I got when I put a little pressure on the line to see if the trout was still on, then the thrill as a hard rod yank stung the hook home and the unseen trout splashed mightily under the bank before being drawn clear, to swing glittering like a rare jewel to the turf.

John McLain on the Roaring Kill.

Now I raised the rod to bring the worm to the surface so I could check its progress. There was a lively boil behind the bait and my line snaked toward a rock. With my heart ticking over, I waited long seconds, then struck. I had caught a good one for the Roaring Kill—9 inches of wild brook trout.

I gave the rod to John McLain, retrieved my beer and rejoined Ed on the bank.

I took a swig of beer, lit my pipe and then lay on my back watching the puffy white clouds drift by. Somehow I got to thinking about the house.

During Prohibition, the late Legs Diamond had a still put in the barn that went with the place, and the bootleggers who worked the still lived in the old house. Their lookout was a woman who lived down the dirt road. Lookout or not, the Revenuers came one day, burned the barn, smashed the still and ripped apart the house somewhat, looking for money perhaps. Ed Lyon and friends became the new owners after the house had lain empty for some years.

Today it is as isolated as the day Legs Diamond first saw it—more so, perhaps, since the orchard is grown up with birch, maple and hemlock now. The Catskill Mountains crowd down on this tiny valley—called Mink Hollow—cut on one side by the Roaring Kill and presided over by the old house.

"Did you guys ever use the power plant?" I asked.

"Nope. I think, after we got it in, we decided it was too civilizing."

With much effort, a concrete slab was poured for the foundation. Then the powerhouse was built. Finally a secondhand generating plant of considerable weight and age was jockeyed into position and a cable was buried leading to the house, some fifty feet away. There is still some crude wiring in the house which, by the way, is a narrow two-story clapboard affair with a brick chimney somewhat out of plumb. The kitchen is at the back in a shedlike room.

From the beginning, the house was lit by kerosene lamps and it still is. The house has resisted change rather successfully. Repairs were made only out of absolute necessity, as when frost-heaves would tumble in part of the fieldstone wall in the dirt-floored cellar.

John McLain came over to join us. "I must be losing my touch. A trout cleaned me three times running. We're out of worms."

We began turning over rocks, finding worms and

Ed Lyon creeling another small brookie for breakfast next morning. McLain holds creel.

chasing small, lively salamanders, which also made
excellent trout bait. Presently we had the bait box
well-stocked and sat back to take it easy.

Absolutely nothing can beat a fine spring day in
the Catskills. You cannot imagine cleaner air, or
greener, fresher buds on the trees, some with that
waxy look they take on just before bursting. The
Roaring Kill ran as pure and clear as it must have a
century ago.

"Look at those wild brookies," I remarked.
"There are damn few left in the East now." We
could see two dimunitive trout finning easily at the
edge of a current, their white-edged lower fins
poised, their tails cocked in the part curl of trout
ready to dash for an insect.

"How do you *know* they're wild?"

Ed Lyon unpacking car at the
house in Mink Hollow.

"Easy. The state doesn't stock them this small. They've always been wild brookies in the Kill."

When we were kids the brook trout was our piscatorial Golden Fleece. To be sure, some rainbows ascended the Roaring Kill from its eventual junction with the upper Schoharie Creek a few miles downstream, but we knew they were fish-truck intruders invading the Kill because of their spring spawning urge.

Catching a "big" brookie—say 10 inches long—was a real event. A fish this size would be fully mature in this brook and able to reproduce. It would also be more than passing wise. To my surprise, I began to remember individual pools where brook trout of this size had made a fatal mistake, and McLain now approached one. Ed and I crowded behind, kibitzing.

This is a "big" brook trout for the Roaring Kill, about 9 inches.

"You're fishing the wrong area," Ed advised. "They're always down at the tail of this pool."

"I can't cast down there without spooking them."

So we let him be, and soon he panicked a fair trout at the tail which shot forward with a zigzag wake. McLain moved to the next pool.

"What's with that toilet on the way down to the cellar?" I asked. I'd wanted to see how the walls were holding up below, opened the door and nearly tripped over a john.

"It was the gals—they didn't like the old one."

"Hell, that's still the finest throne in the Catskills."

"I always thought it was."

This shack is situated on a little bluff over-looking the Roaring Kill. It is conventional in most

Best brookies caught one morning on the Kill.

ways except that it has a plate-glass door on swing hinges which faces the stream. Inside, nailed to one wall, an enameled plaque advises all that a Dr. Wharton can cure virtually all venereal diseases known to man.

The fine thing about this john was that you could sit there looking through the glass door and watch anyone who happened to be fishing the Kill. Someone once saw a deer from within, I understand. Also, if anyone came by, all he had to do was look through the glass to see if the place was occupied. But some female must not have appreciated the charm of this arrangement.

We eased down the brook, leaving no trout hiding place unprobed.

Eventually it was Ed's turn again. "Remember the day we fished Platte Clove?" McLain remarked. "*That* was a mistake!"

We had climbed down a 45-degree slope to get at a remote brook tumbling over great boulders and foaming into spectacular pools. The trouble was that these falls were just steep enough to prevent trout from ascending and the brook was barren.

It grew hot. McLain opened the creel and there was lunch—withered "rat" cheese and a stale loaf of bread. We choked some down and by evening finally worked our way to the floor of the valley, still troutless.

Then the alpine climb up the road. Unbelievable. At Mike Curran's bar in Tannersville I drank the most beer of my life at one sitting—seventeen. And still I was thirsty.

We talked about the time I made a crazy bet with McLain that I could catch a trout in the Roaring Kill in the dead of winter. I forget what the payoff was to be if I failed. But I do remember

John McLain with a small brookie on the Kill.

the drifts across the dirt road, and the struggle we had getting the car through them and over the last rise before the downhill stretch to the house.

I also remember the unrelenting cold in the house, with the thermometer at the kitchen-sink window standing at around fifteen-degrees below zero. We didn't have sleeping bags in those days, and there were never enough blankets in the place. Furthermore, we weren't equipped with clothing that was really warm. I recall that John wore a football helmet with a towel under it.

Well, I had read somewhere—Jack London, perhaps—that you could catch trout through the ice on uncooked bacon, so off we set down the Roaring Kill, me with a fly rod, reel, line, and bare hook on a short leader. I kept the bacon in my pocket so it would stay limber.

The big trouble was unexpected—the brook was frozen over! You could hear it chuckling away under the ice, but you could walk right over the main current, sidestepping the drifts. What we were doing was illegal at the time, but we solved this problem by agreeing that *if* I caught a trout, I would release it promptly.

Down the Kill we stumbled, wishing we had snowshoes but determined to find some open water. I put forward the notion that if the brook was iced over for a mile, we ought to quit and that all bets would be off.

McLain would have none of this. "You'll fish if I have to chop a hole in the creek," he said. Relentlessly, he led the search for some open water.

And eventually, deep among the hemlocks, we came upon an opening in the Kill. It didn't happen to be an opportune place for fishing—it was in the middle of a fast riffle—but there was a pool below locked under the ice and just to get the entire shambles over with, I drew the bacon from my pocket and impaled a dirty wad of it on the hook.

The current swept this offering under the ice, drawing it downstream to the pool. I felt what I thought was a nibble and struck, then reeled in interminably. In time a 5-inch brookie appeared, so cold it could hardly wiggle. Indeed, I didn't know it was on during the retrieve. We took a picture, released the trout and trudged back, wondering just what we were going to do with the rest of that frigid weekend.

Thinking back on it now, I believe I recall what the bet was—if I caught a trout, I wouldn't have to wash the dishes.

It was great being kids in those pre-television days. Time was endless; worries unknown. No one had any money but that hardly mattered. Some of this feeling of absolute freedom came to us now as we entered that part of the Roaring Kill deep in the woods before you reach the iron bridge. There are long pools here, and some deep ones too. In places it is even possible to cast a fly.

I was fishing again. We had finished our beer and buried the last set of cans. We'd had no lunch and it was now midafternoon, but no one spoke of turning back. The challenge of the little trout, the fun of fishing with worms again after all these years, the ordinary pleasure of walking down the Kill in solitude, these elements drew us on and on.

I came to a certain pool and recalled a time of triumph. I was then just starting to fish with flies and had never caught a decent trout on a dry fly. It seemed that was a mystery that I'd never master. Anyhow, I came to this pool fishing by the instruction book—tapered line, a nine-foot leader ending in the lightest wisp of gut, and on the end a No. 12 Dark Cahill.

The pool seemed empty. I made a cast anyhow from the bottom of it, so the fly would float toward me without drag. Midway, over an open gravelly bottom, a trout rose to intercept the fly. It was like a dream as the spotted brookie stuck its nose above the surface and clamped on the fly. How savage that trout was! I could see it run along the bottom, rubbing its jaw against the pebbles as it tried to dislodge the fly.

I spoke out loud to this trout, entreating it to behave. When it made for a sunken bush I just managed to keep the fish clear. And eventually— just as in the books—I drew it swimming weakly to me and beached it on a tiny spit of sand. I had caught a patriarch of the Roaring Kill—a whopping 13-incher—by artificial means in the most sporting tradition and that one incident, more than any other, made a lifelong fly fisherman of me.

This time, I caught a 5-incher on a worm and dropped it into the creel.

A couple of hundred yards farther along, we quit. Ed Lyon, the most thorough and persistent worm angler I ever saw, didn't draw a touch from three lovely pools and we decided the Kill had been penetrated from below by others to this point. So we climbed the steep banks, shouldering aside the beeches till we hit the dirt road leading to the old house.

It was cool inside, with front and back doors open. I threw together some sandwiches and then we sat around the kitchen table relaxing. A couple of corks had been pulled and that helped.

Above the table hung the antique kerosene chandelier. On the wall behind me reposed the charcoal nude, just a touch suggestive and definitely a work of art, that Hugh Laidman had done so many years ago. The "new" pump at the sink—perhaps seventeen years old now—still drew clear, cold water from the dug well directly below in the cellar. And there was still a good wood and coal-burning kitchen range, courtesy of Sears, Roebuck, and about of the same vintage as the pump.

I looked idly at the ceiling. "What happened to the bullet hole?" I asked.

"It's still there," Ed said. "The ceiling's a little dirty, that's all."

I glanced out the back door and caught the glint of the Roaring Kill. *How little it changes here,* I thought.

Suddenly remembering the trout, I got up and put them in a big plastic bag and set them inside the icebox. Not one was over 9 inches but this didn't matter at all. McLain lit up a twisty, black cigar. Ed Lyon lounged in a rickety chair, twirling his whiskey glass.

"Fishing the Kill with only one rod is the absolute answer," John remarked. "No hurrying to get past somebody. Every pool gets fished. We were together."

That was partly why it had been so great. That and the unchanged Roaring Kill, starting at a spring on the hillside to the left of the Notch and flowing down through Mink Hollow, clear and just a bit noisy, with just enough wild brook trout to keep you going from pool to pool.

II

PROBLEMS OF THE WEST

Strangest Trout Lake in the West

THE FIRST TIME I saw Henrys Lake, which lies in a mountain basin in Idaho a little west of Yellowstone National Park, I thought: *It's finished till fall.* The water was as green as pea soup from "working." I stuck my finger in. Warm. Far too warm for trout fishing. The brilliant August sun blasted out of a cloudless sky and made heat waves shimmer on the surface.

Then a fish rose out in the middle. . .

One recent spring I returned—"spring" being early June, a few days after the season opened—and I thought: *We're too damned early.* It was snowing hard. Winds of maybe 25 knots ripped the length of the lake. Huge waves crashed. The thermometer quivered at 39 degrees as we struggled to put up the tent. But I was wrong again. Henrys is worth fishing whenever you can get to it, particularly if you're a fly fisherman, and its lessons have helped me wherever I've had to fish "blind" to unseen trout.

But be prepared for this—it is different. Consider the first day I fished it that August with Ted Trueblood. We'd run down the length of the lake from the public campground and were now anchored within shouting distance of Stayley Spring. A dozen or more boats were anchored nearby, with most of their occupants fly fishing, although one or two used spinning gear.

A huge trout rolled between us and another boat. But no one looked or made a cast toward the spot.

"They're rising," I said excitedly.

"They usually are," Ted replied, busy with his tackle. "Big trout are all around us."

I'd been searching the surface to see what sort of fly the fish had taken, but the only living creatures I saw were, of all things, a few snails floating.

"What do they rise to?" I said impatiently.

"Don't know." Ted got out a cast before I happened to see what he was using. "Whatever it is, no one catches them on dry flies."

"Then what do you use?"

"Nymphs."

He handed me a box of them. Most were short and hairy. As I was examining them, Ted said, "They're shrimp imitations, mostly. Lift out a wad of weeds floating near the shore and you'll find it crawling with shrimp or daphnia. There are some May flies and others, too, but mostly we use shrimp nymphs."

I put on one and cast it out and jerked the line so it would sink. A man in a boat 100 yards away sprang into life with a fish that put a glittering curve in his fly rod.

Soon a jolt ran through the canoe as Ted set the hook in a trout. Hurriedly I got in my line. The fish fought strongly and deep, like a bass trying to get in a hole among rocks. A few minutes later Ted got it to the surface, there was a wild flurry, and it was gone again. But the next time up the trout was manageable and Ted soon netted a fat 4-pound cutthroat—a beautiful fish with the characteristic scarlet slashes beneath the jaws.

I'd never seen a cutthroat as big and said so.

"Standard Henrys Lake size," he said calmly. Then he unhooked it, held it up a moment to admire it, and quickly slipped it back into the water.

"Supper!" I cried. "You've thrown back our supper!"

"Oh, we don't eat cutthroats when the water's this green. Only brook trout."

"Don't tell me you catch brookies like that here?"

"Sometimes. The big ones usually break off. But two or three or four pounds is a good brookie for eating."

Cutthroat trout are commonest in Henrys Lake, where fish like this one are often released when water is green.

The big ones usually break off, I repeated to myself. Another heavy trout rolled nearby and as

before, no one looked. I searched among the
boats—two men were playing fish. The others all
wore looks of deep concentration.

"What's a good day's catch?" I asked.

"Earlier in the week I came over here with Gary
Howells. When we quit just before noon we'd
caught twenty-eight."

I sat there figuring. They had caught probably
100 pounds of trout before noon.

Ted pointed his rod at a spot near the lodge
perhaps 200 yards away by the lake edge. "That's
Staley Spring," he said. "Some years ago spin
fishermen discovered the trout were so thick there
they could snag fish merely by letting a lure sink
and giving it a yank when it got to the bottom. But
the Fish and Game Department put a stop to that.
They closed the area and strung barbed wire
through it besides."

Another trout rose.

A man in a boat nearby gave a shout and a wave
to someone on shore as he struggled with a trout.

"We're sitting at the edge of a channel," Ted
said. "The bottom is muddy and there are weeds
down there. You have to let the line and nymph
sink deep enough so that when you retrieve the
nymph moves just above the weeks."

I tried it, and got weeds every time. Finally I
said, "All right. How do you do it?"

"I count off the seconds while the line sinks. If I
catch weeds on a thirty-second line sink, I cut her
back to twenty-five or whatever until I get it right.
The fish I just caught was a twenty-second trout
and that's how I'm working it right now."

In the next half hour I made twenty-second
casts in every direction but got no encouragement.
Meanwhile, Ted hooked and later released another

Author with a hefty rainbow-
cutthroat "cross" trout at
Henrys Lake, Idaho.

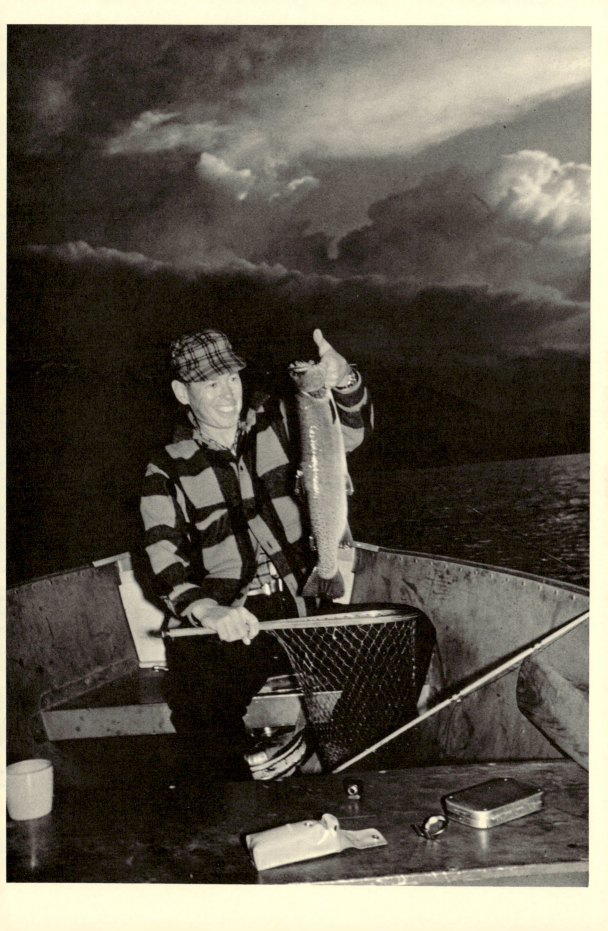

fat cutthroat and fishermen in other boats caught trout. I began to feel a little desperate. I was using the same nymph as Ted, the same length and diameter of leader, and cast in the same general area. Finally, after the canoe had rocked to the hooking of yet another trout—not by me—I got a thrill.

Just as I lifted the nymph clear of the water for another cast, a broad spotted tail slapped the water beneath the dangling fly and there was a great upheaval. Immediately the tiredness left my bones. I noticed that it was a beautiful day, if hot. I admired a white pelican swinging in lazy circles high in the sky.

Then I remembered something I learned fishing for Atlantic salmon several years ago. It sounds screwy but it has to do with faith. A salmon

Ted Trueblood with typical Henrys Lake trout, a rainbow-cutthroat hybrid or "cross."

doesn't rise to a fly out of hunger; it almost has to be beckoned. You have to believe that your salmon fly is the most tantalizingly beautiful thing ever to be put into the river. Then you—or I, at least—begin to catch fish. Anyhow, I now concentrated this sort of feeling toward the nymph. I told myself that it was an irresistible morsel dodging among the weeds and that as soon as a passing trout happened to see it——

Fifteen minutes later I hooked my first Henrys Lake cutthroat, an insignificant 2-pounder but a most satisfying trout just the same. A little reluctantly, I turned it loose.

Later I came to know the four spots where trout are commonly taken in summertime—in front of the lodge and in the channels running into the lake from the mouths of Duck, Targee and Howard

Trueblood playing a Henrys trout, most of which are caught on nymphs, though some take Mickey Finn streamers or steelhead flies.

creeks. Of them all, I liked Duck best because of the challenge. It is laced liberally with dead willows and can be frustrating, as I found out that afternoon.

Ted shut off the kicker a couple of hundred yards out and we picked up the paddles for a silent approach. I could see trout rising when the dead willows were still more than 100 yards away. Presently we were tied to a willow whose tips just poked above the surface.

"It's shallower here," Ted said. "You shouldn't need to count much more than ten or twelve."

We were at the edge of a pocket in the willows about fifty feet wide and twice as long. A trout rose smack in the middle and I thought: *That's for me.* I cast. Ted cast nearby. He caught it. But I didn't really want that fish (a 2½-pound brookie, fat and sleek, which we kept for supper). I had only driven 2,600 miles to get to this spot, gotten up at 4 A.M. that morning, missed my breakfast and spilled half a cup of hot tea on my ankle as we got set to catch these trout.

I didn't really care. But I did manage to get out a cast to the next riser before Trueblood was ready. I missed it and hung the nymph in the willows.

"Break it off but try to remember the branch it's on," Ted said.

I came to know several willows—both above and beneath the water—quite well. I also became acquainted with various sturdy weed growths. There was an ascending clump near my end of the canoe and once I had the pleasure of seeing—for the water was clearer here—a brookie suddenly appear behind my nymph as it "struggled" upward to take it. The trout never hesitated. He took it in one smooth, curving dash and was firmly hooked. But the fish—which would have been brought home in honor back East—weighed only about 1½ pounds and I turned it loose.

In a little more than half an hour we had lost about a dozen flies in the willows but had hooked or caught eight trout, mostly brookies, and I felt I was beginning to get the hang of it. A cast near a rise often brought a strike, but a blind cast near weeds was often just as productive. It had become the most natural thing for me to make a cast, sit staring at the second hand of my watch and then begin to retrieve in a state of increasing excitement. The strikes usually were firm but delicate— almost like hooking a fragile weed.

"It's time we picked our flies off the willows and moved," Ted said presently. "But first, why don't you catch the trout in that little pocket in the willows?"

I had seen the fish boiling up in there repeatedly. The opening was only about a yard wide and

An evening's production of nymphs for Henrys, stuck on a heel of bread overnight to allow drying of varnish on the heads.

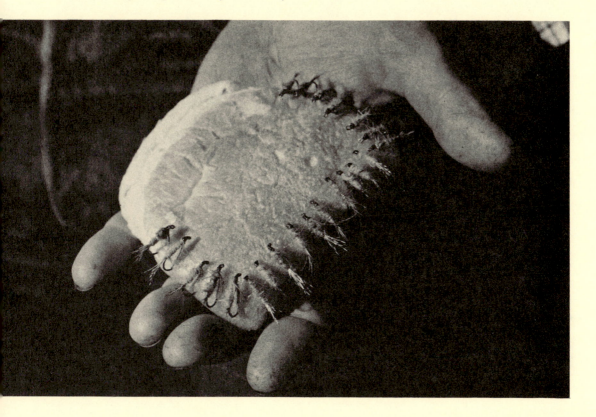

not much longer. Knowing I'd have to horse the fish, I cut back the leader a couple of strands to stronger monofilament and made a cast.

"Don't let it sink much." warned Ted.

I started to work the nymph and the trout struck hard. Immediately I hauled back on the rod. Man! Cutthroats ordinarily don't jump. This one came flying. He shot out of his lair and dived under the canoe into my bank of weeds. Before I got the slack organized he was out again and charging for a half-submerged willow. I just barely got the fish turned away.

Now the trout ran into open water. I opened my mouth to say something thankful when it doubled back for the willows, did a wild surface dance around the nearest branch and was free.

Trueblood netting a trout in Henrys near a sunken creek marked by dead willows in background.

The whole affair had taken ten seconds. Maybe less.

"The big ones always act like that in here," Ted said. "If you use a leader heavy enough to hold them they won't hit. All you can do is swallow your palate and hold on."

I guessed the weight of my rambunctious cutthroat at 4 pounds. What would a 5- or 6-pounder be like?

As we prospected from opening to opening, I soon realized that this was the best lake fishing I had ever seen. And the easiest. For there are none of the problems so often found fishing a mountain lake (Henrys sits a bit below Targee Pass—elevation 7,300 feet—on the Continental Divide). You don't have to wait for a hatch of flies for the fish to bite because they don't take them off the surface. And you don't have to worry about the trout being skittish because of ultraclear water.

However, there are those dead willows. At the next pondlike opening, Ted hooked a fish in the middle which promptly made for the nearest clump. The trout pulled line through Ted's restraining fingers with relentless power. Soon the fish stopped. Ted raised the rod.

"Damn, he hung the fly on a limb. That was a good fish."

"Know what it was?"

"It felt like a brookie. Henrys has so many the Fish and Game Department has a facility here to net them in the fall and take their spawn. As I understand it, Idaho gets all its brook-trout eggs from Henrys Lake and they take some from cutthroats, too. But not from rainbows. There aren't many pure rainbows in here because they crossbreed with cutthroats."

Henrys is partly man-made. A dam was built some years ago to raise its natural level. That's why there are dead willows at the creek mouths—the new water level killed them off. The lake is tremendously fertile and must support a prodigious amount of insect life. Every bunch of weeds or grass I picked up along the shoreline literally dripped nymphs and leeches and the pale, shrimp-like scuds.

Fortunately, Henrys' fertility seems destined to perpetuate good fishing because of its weed crop. By summer vacation time, great masses of them have climbed to the top or just beneath it, so that it is impossible to troll the lake—weeds foul the motors and lures quickly. So in summertime, when fishing is best, the lake is by no means crowded. Apparently there just aren't many fly fishermen in the area, and spinning produces only mediocre results then. Except for the channel in front of the lodge—where there were often several boats—we practically had the lake to ourselves.

Even so, it didn't take long that afternoon for us to try all the openings in the Duck Creek willows that looked promising. By then I'd lost track of the fish and what a wonderful feeling it was. So we decided to run down to the public campsite at the far end of the lake (about four miles) and get our legs unkinked, eat, and then try the Howard Creek channel from the campground beach.

"It is good?" I asked, thinking of its accessibility.

"Well, my wife caught a cutthroat there that went seven and a half. It's usually worth fishing."

Later, off the beach, more trout bit the inno-cent-looking nymphs. They were played, hefted, admired, photographed and put back. By now I was thoroughly won by Henrys Lake. I had never seen so many worthwhile trout in a day's fishing. Not a one weighed less than 1¼ pounds and several were around 3 or over. Still, according to Ted, the day was only so-so compared to what Henrys could deliver.

We fished the lake four times that August and each time I came away bug-eyed. Even so, we never hit it just right, which is why I went back the next June. "The lake will be a lot different then," Ted had written me. "We ought to slaughter them."

Ah, springtime at Henrys Lake. The gales blew and the snow and rain flew. We camped at the public campground and were often lulled to sleep by the crashing of waves on the beach. The facilities were good—a dock, concrete ramp for backing trailers into the water, john, garbage pails—and we aimed to be close to the fishing when the wind would let us on the lake.

One morning when we got up, it was flat calm and the sun was shining. We had a hurried breakfast, made some lunch and roared down the

Trueblood playing trout hooked near dead willows marking channel of an old creek flooded when lake was dammed.

lake toward the lodge. Previous excursions had shown us that the trout were not in their summer-time haunts by the creek mouths and now we were off to try an area which trollers had reported to be productive.

Plainly, the lake was different in the spring. The water was clear, for one thing. And the weed level was quite low, for another. Most of the fishermen we saw were trollers and there were a lot more of them than in the summer. On our last Saturday there were dozens of cars at the campground. Each had a trailer. The variety of the boats amazed me. Outboard cruisers of sixteen feet and more were commonplace. There were actually some fairly large *inboard* cruisers. They plied the lake at snappy speeds, blew air horns in greeting and communicated with one another by two-way radio.

And they caught trout.

There was a stretch out in the middle that produced well for them. But the area we were bearing down on in Ted's fourteen-foot aluminum boat was a reach of the lake in the vicinity of the lodge which we had never tried before. Soon we were fishing.

The lake was beautiful. Fresh snow lay along the ridges of the mountains that ring this end of Henrys. The air was so clear that landmarks stood out with a theatrical effect.

"Here comes the wind," Ted said presently.

Farther down the lake whitecaps began to appear. We cast anxiously and kept changing flies. Ted told me that bucktails and standard wet flies—particularly those with yellow dominating their patterns—were sometimes just as good as nymphs. We hadn't used them last summer because there was no need to, but now we tried them methodically.

rueblood netting a trout at
Ienrys. Stayley Springs and
he lodge are in background,
eft.

A cloud crossed the sun. I glanced at my anchor rope; we were dragging. Then I picked the right fly (yellow body and long gray hackles) and cast to the right spot and let it sink just the right length of time.

"I got one!" I said happily.

The trout started away slowly. I put pressure on it to keep it away from some weeds I could see.

"He's strong," I said.

I raised the rod in hope of getting a look at the fish and felt it start up. Perhaps it saw the bottom of the boat, or the white anchor ropes. Anyhow, it suddenly bolted, tearing the line out of my fingers and then off the reel in a rising shriek. I tried braking the flowing line lightly with my fingers but this was a trout beyond stopping.

Abruptly the run faltered. I raised the rod and was unable to move the fish. And then what was a first just a horrible thought became fact—the trout had flung itself deep into a patch of weeds and broken off.

Ted put on a Mickey Finn bucktail and went to work with it while I looked dazedly for another fly. How big had my trout been? Five pounds? Eight? A troller had told us of losing a big trout near his boat that he swore would have gone better than 10 pounds. Clearly mine had been bigger than any I had hooked so far.

A few minutes later Ted hooked a trout that put a deep bow in his rod as it took line. I reeled in hurriedly to give him a clear field and took what bearings I could so we could find this area again, for we were still drifting every now and then with both anchors out.

"He's a good one," Ted said finally. "I can't get him to come up at all."

Trueblood unhooking a
Henrys Lake trout.

It was a pleasure to watch that struggle. For a long ten minutes neither of us glimpsed the trout. And then it permitted itself to be brought up just far enough for a good look.

We both started shouting at once. It was a brook trout—the fattest and longest I had ever seen. It was so thick that it seemed to waddle instead of swim. It took Ted another five minutes to get it to the top again. And when at last he had netted it, unhooked it, tapped the back of its head and laid it out on the center seat, I still could not take my eyes off it to start fishing again. The trout weighed a thumping 5¼ pounds. It was as regal and wild-looking as a salmon.

A spit of rain rattled against the boat as we started to fish again. Only two of the middle-of-the-lake trollers remained. Ted started the motor and ran us back to where he'd hooked the brookie and we flailed out casts against the wind. But it was no use. The boat drifted against the anchors so fast we couldn't work our flies properly and we decided to quit while we could still navigate the four miles back to camp.

The fishing at Henrys remained chancy. One evening the wind quit a little before sundown and we raced down to the lodge to find several trout rising quietly a couple of hundred yards out from the dump. In half an hour we had three, one a 4-pound cutthroat Ted caught just as the sun went down. Then it pinched out. A cold wind sighed down out of the mountains, freshened to a moan and we had to race home.

"You'd think the damned fish could bite a little closer to camp," Ted grumbled.

One day, fishing the South Fork of the Madison not far away, we counted no less than eight storms that swept across the mountains that lie just to the north of Henrys. The wind was pretty fresh on the South Fork too, but not so bad that you couldn't fish it. That night on the way to the lake for a bucket of water, I passed two fellows sitting by their campfire.

"Weather pretty sour today?" I asked them.

"You didn't miss a thing," one of them said.

But the lake did give us half a day after almost two weeks of frustration. It was almost as if it knew we'd have to break camp the next morning and it outdid itself along about noon. The clouds cleared away and the lake began to calm nicely.

We ran down to the big brook trout hole but there was nothing doing. Then we tried it off the dump and Ted caught a trout but that was that; it seemed to be a loner.

"Let's drift," I said. It was warm enough for shirtsleeves and bright enough to get a tan. Only the gullys below the peaks had snow left now. A hatch of May flies began to come off the lake.

"No use copying them," I said. "Henrys' Law."

"Look, the water has started to turn green," Ted remarked. "I'll bet the good fishing will start next week when you're back in Connecticut."

A faint breeze took us toward Duck Creek. Here and there I noticed some weeds had reached the surface. We made fifteen-second casts out each side of the boat. It seemed almost too easy, without the wind.

"I got one," I said presently. "But he's not very big."

"A fish is a fish," said Ted as he dropped the stern anchor.

It was a 2-pound cutthroat, a pretty fish and a lively one. I thought: *Where else can you catch trout like this?* and I let the cutthroat fight as long as it could take line off the reel.

"Do you realize we are almost off the mouth of Duck Creek?" Ted said. "I believe they're headed back for the willows at last."

Presently Ted caught one and the tension began

to build. It was screwy, sitting there counting out
the seconds. The chances of catching fish seemed
so remote, working those colorless little nymphs
down there in the gloom among the weed stems.

Yet it *was* working. And we were going to take
eight trout before the afternoon was over. We
didn't know this, of course. You never do when
you fish blind, counting out the seconds and then
psyching yourself to believe that this retrieve will
bring a strong fish.

The Method That

Revolutionized Fly Casting

THE FELLOW IN the other boat was making amazing casts. His yellow fly line would soar out over Henrys Lake, in northeast Idaho, and come to rest lightly on the water far, far away. He was casting eighty or ninety feet, maybe one hundred. And he made it look easy, far easier than the 50- or 60-foot casts I was driving out with all my might. He'd pick up his line from the water with a backward toss of his rod and then get this tremendous forward distance *with no false casting.*

I had to find out how he did it, and moved closer to watch. What I learned, beginning that day several seasons ago, has improved my lot as a fly fisherman in so many ways that I'm still astonished when I think about it.

The fellow at Henrys Lake had taken a double-taper line, a standard ninety-footer, and cut it off a third of the way back from one end. This made a thirty-foot line, tapered at the front end. He then whipped a loop of heavy, braided dacron surf line to the thick end and attached it to one hundred feet of twenty-pound-test monofilament, which in turn was tied to regular backing line.

As he retrieved, the caster let the monofilament fall on the floorboards of his boat in big coils. He brought in the monofilament until it pulled a short length of the fly line through the tip guides. Then he made a backcast—without releasing line—and drove the rod forward powerfully, releasing his left-hand grip on the monofilament as the fly line shot forward.

The coils of light, slick monofilament snaked up off the floorboards, shot through the guides and the fly flew on and on. Then the last bit of monofilament jumped tight against the rod and pulled a few clicks from the reel.

With only two rod motions, this man had belted out a cast such as I'd never in my life made, even with a wind at my back. It was like watching a golfer make a hole-in-one and knowing it was going to happen beforehand.

I was watching one of the early users of shooting tapers or heads, often called just *heads*. Western tournament casters developed this idea and then the steelheaders adapted it to fishing. But there is more to using heads than just making long casts. I couldn't make 90-foot casts when I started later that day. But right away I discovered an advantage I'd not suspected. I was casting from the beach below the public campground at Henrys Lake. An old stream channel parallels the shoreline there, and you need to make a cast of at least sixty feet to fish the area properly. I looked around to check backcast room and groaned. No long cast could escape that sagebrush.

Then I remembered I didn't need a 50-foot backcast to make a 60-foot forward cast. If I flipped back only 25 feet of fly line, the rest shot through the guides on the forward cast and pulled out the monofilament I'd coiled on the beach at my feet.

But it seemed to me that I was still less efficient

than the fellow on the lake. I figured something must be wrong. And I was right. I'd cut off a thirty-foot section from the double-taper line that worked well with my rod. This was a basic mistake, as I learned later, for the line was now too light for the rod.

Basically a fly rod casts *weight*, and double-taper lines are comparatively heavy. A typical medium-weight floating line—the customary ninety feet long—weighs 482 grains, which is more than one ounce. When I make a cast and work out half this line, I'm keeping aloft something over half an ounce with every false cast. A heavier line is even worse; half of it weighs more than three quarters of an ounce.

I call this work. So does the fly rod.

So someone devised the torpedo-taper or weight-forward line, which was a considerable improvement over the double taper in some respects. The weight-forward line has a forward portion of fairly heavy line which tapers back to a small-diameter "running" line. You work out the heavier line beyond the tip and then shoot it out. It pulls out running line that's either held in big, loose coils in the left hand or coiled on shore or boat bottom.

But a weight-forward line is really good for only one thing—making long casts. It won't make decent roll casts, and it doesn't perform well on short to medium-length casts. Then heads came along in the late 1950's and gave anglers another option. Heads were still so new in the summer of 1958 that only Scientific Anglers made a short line designed to be tied to monofilament and cast with a fly rod, and it was a sinking line, no doubt intended for steelhead fishing. All other shooting heads in use were homemade.

What a head does, of course, is save casting weight, and the monofilament it trails weighs only one grain a foot, *a sixth of what size D fly line weighs*. Heads for moderately powerful rods weigh about 230 to 260 grains.

It was a thrilling experience to use a shooting head of the right weight on my second day at Henrys Lake. Casting suddenly became downright easy. Because I was reaching much farther—up to 80 feet or so, counting my 10-foot leader—I was fishing more on every cast. I had to make myself keep fishing because I was continually tempted to make long casts just for the fun of it.

After this Western vacation ended, I began using heads in the East and discovered all sorts of unexpected advantages. The first is quite obvious: one double-taper line yields two heads, and so will a torpedo taper if it has a long, heavy casting section. (They vary greatly from maker to maker, but most firms have catalogs that give detailed line measurements.) Because you have only thirty feet or so of fly line on a reel instead of ninety, there's room for a lot more backing line under the monofilament.

My casting heads are much easier to tote. I used to carry an extra reel that held a sinking line but now I just carry an extra head or two. They make up easily into four-inch coils which I secure with short twists of pipe cleaner. I use a small cardboard tag on a short rubber band to identify each head: its weight, length, whether it's a floater or a slow or fast sinker.

Changing heads on a stream is so easy that I now do something I rarely bothered with when I carried a spare reel. If I come to a stretch of water that needs to be fished with a wet fly, when I've been fishing a dry, I switch heads. You can do this without wading ashore.

Another thing I learned is that a head, because of its higher velocity, is much easier to drive into

Ted Trueblood of Nampa, Idah casting a shooting head for sal on a brook near Portland Creek, Newfoundland.

the wind than a conventional fly line. After trying heads from 28 feet all the way to 35 I've settled on the length of 30 feet as being best for all-round use. For bad wind I have a 28 and a 29 footer that I made from heavy torpedo-taper lines. These short heads "turn over" well and will bore into a vicious headwind beautifully.

The important thing about a head is that its weight must be correct to bring out the action of a particular rod, which is no problem these days when heads are commercially available in 30-grain increments up to about 330 grains. Scientific Anglers label its heads according to the AFTMA designations—7 weight, 8 weight, etc.—to balance rods that are similarly numbered, thus removing the guesswork that plagued makers of homemade heads.

I was using only wet flies in my early experiments. But a head after all is thirty feet of the type of line long considered unbeatable for dry-fly fishing. Add a nine-foot leader and you have a 39-foot cast that will drop a dry fly as delicately as was ever done with a double taper. That 39-foot cast is long enough for most dry-fly work. And you can shoot out much longer casts with a dry fly and still get fairly delicate delivery and good accuracy.

But here's a sensational feature I discovered by accident. I wanted to fish a run on the far side of a big river, and there was the usual problem of sudden drag from the middle current, which was faster. Ordinarily, this cast gives the fly a float of only two or three seconds before drag spoils it.

I waded out as far as I dared, made my cast, and then raised the rod to be in a position to strike instantly. But when I raised the rod I also lifted the light monofilament clear of the middle current, something I hadn't planned to do. I got an eight or nine-second float. I'd lucked upon a way to beat drag on cross-current casts.

Later I happened on something equally valuable. A fish was rising quite a distance downstream in a position that was practically unassailable. He couldn't be reached from below because he was working in front of a bush sticking out halfway across the stream. And he was too far below me to reach with a float because drag would surely spoil it. Or was he? I made a long cast, halted it in midair so it fell in an S on the surface, and began feeding monofilament through the guides.

I expected the line to start dragging quickly, but I hadn't thought of the ease with which monofilament glides through the guides. The fly went downstream without drag, and I caught the trout.

As a result of this happy experience, I now look for spots that can only be fished in this way. Quite often they contain good fish, because anglers with conventional fly lines can't reach them.

Before I go further, a word or two about monofilament running line. I tried various diameters from .015 to .024 and found the best to be .018, .019 and .020 (commonly the diameter of twenty-pound test). However, the perfect mono for running line has yet to be made and casters make a constant search for their ideal. Such a line should not be too stiff, nor should it be too limp. Mono that develops tight curls from being on the reel is hopeless.

My favorite brand is Maxima, made in Germany. Lately, I've heard that Corland's Cobra is excellent but I haven't tried it yet.

Whatever kind you use, cut off and discard the forward yards that fray or develop kinks. The latter can be worked out of the mono somewhat by drawing the kink hard over the rod's grip, or through a piece of folded-over inner tube. Sometimes stretching the line a yard at a time is helpful. Also, there are casting baskets these days for holding your running line while wading deep.

Finally, some makers now have thin, level fly line intended for use as running line. You won't get the distance that you'll get with monofilament but you'll have no kinking or curling problems and these .029-inch lines float, which is handy when making long casts on a shallow lake. Getting your monofilament wet as soon as you go fishing—even if you have to dunk the reel occasionally at the start—goes a long way toward keeping it straight. I tie it to the line, incidentally, by a simple jam knot made with six turns. Because .020 is fairly heavy, this knot holds well and never loosens.

Though I buy ready-made heads these days, I still make up my own when I want some in-between weight to suit a certain rod. Thus, a favorite dry-fly rod is seven feet long and requires a head of *exactly* 210 grains (most rods aren't so fussy). Here's how I go about making a head.

With a dial micrometer I check to see how much level line there is at the front end of a new double-taper line. This level section may vary between two and perhaps, five or six feet. I cut it back to two feet and then measure off 32 or 33 feet of the remaining front half of the line. Usually, the 32 or 33 feet of head line is too heavy, so I start cutting back six inches at a time from the thick, heavy end and weighing after each cut. Some heads come out at 28½ feet, or, say 29¼ feet. No matter; it's weight the rod casts, and heads from 27 to 32 feet will work, though I prefer a head on the short side for a small rod like the seven-footer.

Having cut the line back to the desired weight less two or three grains, I cut a five-inch piece or fifty-pound-test braided casting line (weight: a grain and a half) from a spool, put the ends together and lay the butt of the head between the legs of the proposed back loop. Then with a fly-tier's bobbin I whip the loop on hard with silk or Nymo thread, and varnish it. The whipping and varnish (two coats, a day apart) add a final grain. And while this may sound complicated, it is easy to cut a head and whip a loop to it in ten or fifteen minutes.

There is just one more thing about shooting heads—some anglers like them heavier than recommended, so be warned that finding the heads to suit your pet rods may take a little trial and error.

But once you're set, the dividends are rich. Imagine only one backcast to belt out an 80- or 90-footer. Or floating a fly under a low bridge that's impossible to cast under. It's true you may sometimes step on your running line or foul it on a bush at some crucial moment. Yet this is the greatest aid to fly fishing there is. You fish longer with less effort. Who ever caught a trout while false casting?

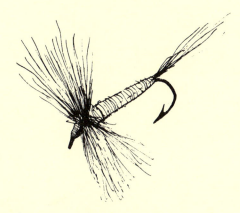

A Lake That Looks Dead Easy

SMOKY MIST STREAMERS climbed slowly above
the lake, and on the far shore the sagebrush lay
blue-green in the early light. Even for an August
morning in the Montana high country, it was
chilly—about 40 degrees. We set the canoe in the
water, and for the first time I noticed how clear
Wade Lake was. A trout came swimming up from
the dark-green depths. As I watched, fascinated,
the fish came close—maybe twenty feet away. I
guessed its weight at about 3 pounds. At that
moment, I fell under a spell from which I never
expect to recover.

For this was at the boat landing; this was where
the campers swam and hung out. Behind us, up the
slope, were a couple dozen tents and trailers that
erupted kids, dogs, and fishermen when the sun
came over the mountain. I'd never seen a trout like
this at a boat landing before.

"Is he tame?" I asked in wonder.

"About as tame as a rattlesnake," Ted Trueblood said. "Why don't you catch him?"

I fumbled my tackle together quickly, salivaed
my leader, and got a cast going. The little fly

settled gently on the surface about ten feet from the trout. If I do say so, it was a nice cast. But the trout bolted wildly.

"Well," said Ted, "they haven't changed any." He sounded a little pleased, but at the same time resigned.

We got into the canoe. Ted started the little outboard fitted on it, and we headed down the shore. Ted had fished Wade many times before.

"There are trout in Wade so big they'll scare you to death," Ted had written to me back East. "Rainbows up to 22 pounds have been taken and browns to around 17. You won't believe it even after you've seen it."

Wade Lake is about two miles long, less than half that wide, and shaped like a mitten. It lies just north of the Continental Divide in Beaverhead National Forest in Montana. It's a lake with a deeply translucent, sparkling look that reflects steep, forested hillsides. You expect to see deer leave the timber to drink in the early morning. Now, as we headed into the thumb-shaped bay, the surface was flat calm. I never saw a trout lake that looked so promising.

Ted cut the motor, and we picked up the paddles. The canoe seemed air-borne as it carried us on crystal water along the edge of a sharp drop-off. A ragged cliff of moss rose from the dark depths, and then fell away perhaps six feet beneath the surface. The water was so clear that as I stared down I could make out a nymph crawling on the swirly green stuff.

A trout suddenly smashed at a bug only a paddle's length from our middle thwart. Another deep fish with a wide tail dived downward.

"Let's try for him," I said excitedly. "He looked like a 6-pounder."

"He saw us," Ted said. "Around here, you have to spot the fish first, not vice versa, and then go to work on him. We'll see one cruising over the moss soon.''

The sun came up and warmed our backs. The mossy shallows became a luminous green. Far down, a fat trout emerged from a cliff cavern, and sailed back in. The lake was silent except for the dropping of water from our paddles as we stared down at the underwater scene. Presently, we came upon a clearing in the moss, a place with a white marly bottom. A big trout lay over the marl, looking as black as an old shoe.

"He's going to see us," Ted said. Then our shadow eclipsed the fish, and when it passed he was gone.

"How big do you think he was?" I asked.

"Six, seven pounds."

Ted Trueblood unhooking a rainbow at Wade Lake. Trout take nymphs at night nearly as well as in daylight. You have to cast blind at night, approximately to where you think the fish will be.

I saw a swirl toward shallow water, and then a trout swimming along.

"He's feeding," Ted said. "Try your little nymph."

I picked up the rod and the trailing line, false cast, and put the nymph about ten feet ahead of the trout. At the last minute, the fish turned, and he never saw the nymph. I waited, hoping he'd come back, but he didn't. Ted backed the canoe as I got set to cast again.

"If you put the fly too close, you'll spook him," Ted said. "But if it's too far away, he won't see it. Makes it nice, eh?"

I cast ahead of the fish again. He didn't spook, but kept coming at the sinking nymph. I crawled it toward me. The trout shot forward a little—he was

Turned free, a trout True-blood caught at Wade swims away.

a rainbow—and then passed over my leader.

"Moss," Ted said. "You've got a thread of moss on your nymph."

But the rainbow was still in sight, and we crept up on him once again. Feeling a little as if I were about to pull the trigger on a record buck, I got off another cast. This time the nymph landed perhaps seven feet from the fish. Instantly the trout bolted from the moss flat.

The day was still chilly, but now I noticed my palms were sweaty. A great excitement took hold of me, and I looked around wildly for another trout.

Trying for them alternately, we continued down the bay. The trout came out of the depths at random to cruise and feed over the moss beds which were riddled with small potholes and caves. We could see the rainbows inspecting them methodically. Now and then a trout prodded his nose into the green stuff for a nymph, or rose ever so gracefully to take a floating fly. These rainbows gave an impression of smooth deftness that was a little frightening. How could you fool them in this goldfish pond of a place?

I cast to my fourth trout. The nymph fell too far away. I cast closer. He swam behind a glob of moss and didn't see it. Then he went off in another direction. Frantically I tried a longer cast, and though in ordinary trout fishing it wouldn't have been alarming, the rainbow burned out of there like a startled bonefish.

I looked at Ted. "We've spooked every trout on this side of the bay," I said. "What now?"

"Guess you haven't noticed that big bunch rising over by that floating moss," he said.

Perhaps a dozen fish were rising; not splashing, just doing a lot of gulping. Now I noticed May flies drifting onto the lake on the lightest of breezes. Without a word, we headed for the trout, paddling

like scared Indians. I eased a rock anchor over-
board, and so did Ted.

What I saw now, broadside to us, gave me the
shakes. The rainbows were in a couple of feet of
water, feeding as if they'd never get enough. I tied
on a No. 16 fly and nervously cast it out toward the
edge of the feeders. Trout zigzagged back and forth
like ants in kerosene. One coasted up to my fly,
glanced at it, and swallowed a natural insect six
inches away.

Ever so carefully, I twitched the line, and for
once the leader sank, but not the fly. A trout swam
idly past my offer and never seemed to notice it.

"Do they ever hit?" I asked in exasperation.

"Right when you least expect it. Moss will fly
six feet in every direction."

We were using 3X leaders about 12 feet long,
and would have used lighter but for the moss. Ted
said that when a fish ran into the moss and
jumped, even 3X would snap like a cobweb. So we
stuck it out, now and then casting to put a fly
where more rainbows would see it.

Soon I noticed there didn't seem to be as many
trout. Had we begun to scare off these fish too?
But it was the hatch: only a couple of dozen May
flies floated now, where there had been hundreds.

I glanced quickly at Ted's fly, taking my eyes
away from my own for a moment, and saw a
rainbow approaching. The fish helped itself to two
May flies that led it down a little alley in the moss
to Ted's. Without a pause or blink, the trout took
Ted's artificial.

Moss flew high, and so did the rainbow—two
vibrant pounds of him, sun-touched and pinkly
gleaming, jumping three feet in twisting terror.

ueblood with a brown
ut at Wade, caught in the
n on a nymph.

"Damn, damn, damn," Ted swore softly. The leap had popped his leader when it came tight against a wad of moss. I felt elated, and at the same time terrible. My eyes ached from staring so long at my tiny fly. Twice I'd lost track of it and struck foolishly when a fish took a natural nearby.

"Give me the coffee," Ted said, and I passed it.

"The breeze will freshen soon," he said presently, staring moodily at the three or four remaining trout. "Then we'll have to try something else."

A rainbow cruised at the edge of the deep water, and I tossed my fly toward him. It was the fifth or sixth pattern I'd tried. At least I could keep track of it easily, out there in the clear. The trout swam underneath it but never looked up. I was beginning to hate them a little, although I continued to stare at them in fascination.

Turning loose a rainbow at Wade. Trueblood stands on a whitish marl flat where fish are easily seen and stalked. Note fall-off to deep water and weeds beyond him.

From somewhere down the lake an outboard started up, and soon we saw the boat, trolling. Ted said trollers seldom do well on Wade because the moss fouls motors as well as lures.

The late Jack Schneider did much toward solving the lake's particular riddles with the invention of his Fledermaus nymph. It's tied with a fuzzed-out body of muskrat-belly fur with some lighter colored fur worked in, giving it a slightly grizzled look. There's a sparse topping of white-tipped, dark brown hair. I noticed that Ted had a large selection that he'd tied from about No. 8 all the way to big, crawly looking No. 2's. Some had heads wrapped with red to identify them as being weighted with lead wire. So far, we hadn't tried anything in the way of a big nymph, and now, of course, we still had our dry flies out there.

Anchored over weeds, Trueblood fishes a Wade Lake marl flat, clearly visible as a light-colored strip.

I looked from the troller to my fly. It was floating by the edge of deep water a yard away from a struggling May fly—the last in the whole area. A rainbow I'd seen time and again—he was much lighter than the others—came along and knocked off the live fly. Then, with no nonsense about it, he took mine—bang.

Ducks flew from the marsh behind when I yelled. It was good to feel the rod jar into life. The trout jumped and ran, sounded, then burst into the air again. He made the leader cut the surface like the prow of a speedboat. I'm not the kind that has to land every trout he hooks, but I found that I wanted this one badly.

The trout took off toward the middle of the lake, and it was a pleasure to let him go and listen to the reel. There was no moss where he went, just plenty of open water. He jumped, and jumped again; then came back, tiring. He came nicely to the net. I put him in a nylon-netting bag slung over the side in the water. Maybe I'd release him later, but just now I wanted to refresh myself with an occasional glimpse at the captive.

By the time we'd boated my trout, all the others had quit rising, and the breeze had freshened just enough to make it difficult to see into the shallows. So we left the bay and headed toward the northwest end of the lake. The breeze blew just right, so we could drift down the shore without paddling, and cast toward it.

There was no moss for quite a stretch. A brief, rocky beach sloped sharply to deep water, but there were plenty of fish-lurking spots in the old dead trees along the shore. We put on weighted nymphs, each a different color, and went to work. There'd be time for a cast and retrieve in little

The mainstay of Wade is rai⟩ bows like this, weighing about 2½ pounds and pack⟩ with vitality.

spurts for about six feet before repeating the procedure.

"There are times," said Ted, "when they'll actually charge a well-worked nymph. You can't take it away from them."

We cast in silence, looking into the deep water but seeing nothing.

"One day," Ted went on, "Jack Schneider and I got into them in the shallows at the other end of the lake. We were wading along the shore. You could see a big one come in, and if you stalked him right, he'd go for the nymph. They were browns mostly. Four and 5- and 6-pounders."

We kept casting like fools, not wanting to let a yard of water go untried. Once Ted started to pick up his nymph for another cast just as a trout darted for the fly. The fish missed, and it was a

All the trout of Wade are wonderful runners and leapers. Here a small rainbow performs for Trueblood.

trout so big that its surface swirl formed a tight light whirlpool that made a sucking sound like water leaving a bathtub.

The memory of that swirl would have carried me through a thousand more casts, but Ted said, "Let's eat. We've been at it more than five hours."

So we beached the canoe and walked to the shade of a spruce. Now it was hot. Heat waves danced over the lake, and we'd long since peeled down to shirtsleeves. We were only about 30 miles from the west entrance of the tourist-crowded Yellowstone National Park, but Wade Lake was so quiet, with such a look of remote wildness about it, it could have been a far-flung lake in British Columbia.

Even as I ate, I found myself watching the lake. Five hours for one trout, and we must have seen a hundred and cast to at least half of them. As I squinted at the sun dancing on the water, I saw a trout splash. Five minutes later, another fish rose. They were out in the deep water, yet feeding on top.

I glanced at Ted. "So you noticed," he said, gulping the last of a sandwich. "I think they're rising to grasshoppers. The wind carries them out there from this high bank."

I found out a few minutes later that he had dry flies specially made up for this occasion—Joe's Hopper or something similar. Still eating, we began to walk the bank and cast out grasshopper flies. There was just enough ripple so you couldn't see into the water. You had to watch for a rise, run down the shore—they never came up where you were, of course—and get out a quick cast. Then you had to wait and hope.

I heard a shout, and saw Ted battling a fish. Then I heard a splash nearby and realized it had been a rise. My fly was under and the fish gone.

Running toward another rise, I saw Ted shake off the trout and make a frantic cast far out onto the lake. Trembling a little, I worked out a cast and concentrated on watching the grasshopper fly. I watched and watched and watched. Then Ted came hurrying along.

"The wind has dropped," he said. "Now is the time to work the moss beds we passed by just before lunch."

We sprinted to the canoe, pitched in our stuff, and paddled out. The light was trickly; at just the right angle you could see clearly, but let the canoe swing around a little, and there was only a tantalizing glare on the surface.

"Stop," I shouted suddenly. I'd seen a big fish emerge from a moss pocket. Somehow, Ted got the canoe halted without changing the angle of view. I cast to the rainbow—one of the big kind that seem to waddle when they swim—with one of Ted's weighted Fledermaus nymphs. It sank beautifully at the edge of the moss bank where the rainbow cruised. He saw it. Never hurrying, he closed on the nymph, and I saw the white of his mouth as he opened up and took it.

I struck, and for one glorious moment felt his heft and his power. Then the nymph came free. I swore. I think the trout had it crossways in his mouth.

The canoe drifted over the shallows until we came to a deep, emerald hole that Ted said was a spring. I held the canoe steady while he sank a nymph in it. With far more patience than I could have mustered just then, he began to inch in line. I pictured the fly-creature struggling off the bottom toward the dappled light above, with Lord only knows how many big trout turning cold, appraising eyes toward it.

Three minutes later I heard Ted catch his breath.

Fishing in the rain, Trueblood hooks a brown trout on a nymph over a marl flat. Another picture in this set shows him unhooking this fish.

Staring hard, for I wasn't in a favorable position, I saw the shadowy form of a large trout angling upward after the nymph.

"The dirty dog," Ted said.

The trout had turned back into the deep hole. It had been at least as heavy as the one I'd hooked a few moments before.

A fitful breeze came up. We didn't want to quit the moss so soon, so we kept at it, staring our eyeballs out. A trout would cruise along, and just as you angled the canoe to cast, the surface would swirl and ruffle just enough to hide the trout. Immediately, six innocent shadows would look like trout and you'd have to wait, rod poised, for the breeze to pass. And when it did, the trout would be gone and you'd have to start all over again.

Ted knew this end of the lake so well he could go from one spot to another without actually being able to see into them. On one such occasion, we drifted the canoe to a point of moss running out into the lake, and the wind suddenly dropped. In less than a minute, it was flat calm.

"There's one," said Ted, casting. The nymph made a tiny splash, and slipped downward on its invisible nylon strand, a bit of barbed deception watched with withering intensity by three pairs of eyes—ours and the trout's. The trout decided that this morsel was heaven-sent. He shot forward and gulped it.

"Look at him jump," said Ted. "Look at the fool run."

That rainbow was pure pleasure. You didn't have to stare and squint and hold the canoe just so. You didn't have to cast as if your nymph were a bomb ready to go off. There was nothing to do but sit there and watch 2½ pounds of vibrant rainbow fight like a gentleman, and wind up in the nylon-mesh bag with the fish I'd put in there hours before.

The wind had come up again, stronger now. We

didn't care. We felt we'd accomplished an excep-
tion feat in taking two of these skittish trout, and
there were several hours left in the day, wind or no
wind.

We drifted down the side of the lake we hadn't
yet fished, and went to work with weighted
nymphs, tossing them beyond the steep drop-off.
This part of the trip was remarkable for two
reasons. One was that for the first time in my life, I
put on a brand-new leader that was rotten, and
weak as straw from end to end. With it I hooked a
brown trout that leaped so close I could have
caught it in my hat. But he broke the leader easily.
The other item was that the lake held me fascinated still, despite growing fatigue that began to
take a grip on my arms and shoulders.

"You tired?" I asked Ted.

"Damn tired. But I know what's coming as soon
as the sun goes down, and it gives me strength. The
lake will be crawling with feeding trout if it gets
calm."

By now we'd drifted to the inlet end of Wade
where moss-draped flats reach out. The breeze
faded, and we saw a few trout again. One rose to a
fly on the surface. Encouraged, we switched to dry
flies. We cast, and just sat there lazily, watching the
fly in the late-afternoon sun. Moreover, because of
the angle of sunlight, our flies were lit up and easy
to see.

A trout took Ted's fly, then burst into a mad
dance of flying spray and bits of moss. He was like
mine; over a pound and absolutely wild. I put him
in with the others. I began to feel energetic and
looked around for a trout to cast to. But something had put them down, or perhaps we happened
on an eager one or two.

"Let's go ashore and stretch our legs," Ted
suggested. "That ought to reassure these fish."

I killed the three trout and photographed them.
Then I soaked my head in the lake. Ted found

some wild raspberries and we ate some. But in the end, it was really the trout that revived us—scores of trout that suddenly began to pockmark the entire end of the lake.

The sun was just going down as we eased the canoe into the shallows and began to cast. Droves of flies floated and danced at the surface. Trout began to slap around on top with the gusto of feeding bluefish. Rapidly I went through several patterns looking for a fly that would murder them.

Trout were so numerous in the gathering dusk that it was impossible to put them down with repeated casts. The lake was dotted with boats now, as frenzied anglers cast to the rising fish. We moved into fresh territory, out over deep water, in case our canoe cast shadows to spook the trout.

The air became chilly and I had to put on a jacket. Though we'd been fishing for 12 hours now, I was as excited as when we'd begun. I looked at Ted. His eyes were red-rimmed and his cheeks had a fallen-in look, but he was smiling.

"You look terrible," I said. "What are you grinning about?"

"Back at camp, Ellen is building the fire she's going to broil the steaks on. You don't look so hot yourself, by the way."

"How do you know we're having steaks?"

"You always need steaks when you fish Wade Lake."

A trout rose 15 feet away, and I cast to it automatically. I sat in hunched aching concentration. Nothing happened. Nothing was happening to fishermen all over the lake, and many began to quit.

"What is this?" I asked finally.

"It's a show they put on so you'll come back," Ted said. "Occasionally you catch a couple in the evening. Oddly, there are evenings when they even take well, but are rare."

When it got so dark you couldn't see to knot on a new fly, we headed for the landing. Trout were still rising. A few stars shone softly.

I knew it was time to quit, and I didn't want to. But I had to. I was beat; just as beat as when I fished Wade a week later—with about the same result.

Ted started the car and turned on the heater before he started struggling with the canoe, which rode on top. I stowed away the other gear. Finally, there was nothing to do but leave with our three fish.

"Will you want to come back?" Ted said.

"Sure," I replied. "I'm hooked for keeps."

"Fine. In that case I can tell you—there are days when you catch nothing but big ones."

A British Columbia Specialty—
Hurry A Fly Downstream

AS WE ROARED down the river in the softness of a May evening, I kept repeating to myself what others had told me about this place. Fred Ludekens, the illustrator, had said, "Without question the finest fly fishing I've found in North America." And then came the clincher back at the airport, where Charley Barfield—returning for his seventh straight season—remarked, "My guide has a standing order to remind me when I've caught and released 50 trout so we can quit and go back to eat."

Fifty trout! And sometimes well before noon!

The boat roared past a riverbank settlement which I took to be the Indian village of Fort Babine and then began to slow on a wide curve. Up ahead I saw a fish rise, and another and another. Presently, as the boat came full into a broad pool several hundred yards long, I saw that it was alive with splashing trout.

For once, the right place at the right time, I thought.

Ted Trueblood and I were fishing now while our guide, host and mentor—Cecil Brown—maneuvered the narrow 25-footer. I remember a solid strike and a feeling of utter disbelief when the trout had popped my stout leader so effortlessly. After that, events merged into a happy daze as hooked rainbows jumped and were either blessed or cursed in despair.

All of a sudden it was nearly dark, and Cecil was wheeling the big boat upriver. I flopped against the foredeck, tired to the bone. . . .

Later, back at our log cabin, we sat around the crackling stove with Cecil Brown and his partner, Ejnar Madsen, who operate their Norlakes Lodge on Babine Lake, B.C., from June 1st into the November hunting season. The Babine River—where we'd recently fished, ten minutes from the lodge by fast boat—is actually the north-flowing outlet and gateway to the sea of this 110-mile lake.

"The fisheries boys say that something like 900,000 sockeye salmon spawned in the Babine River and tributaries of the lake last year," Cecil was telling us, "and laid a fantastic number of eggs. It is their fry—just beginning to hatch out now—that our river rainbows are feeding on."

"What other fish come up from the ocean?" Ted wanted to know.

"We get steelhead runs beginning in mid-September, and four of the five kinds of Pacific salmon. Some of their young—we call the bigger, year-old fish 'migrants'—are also in the river now."

Silence fell upon the cabin for a long moment. A loon called. I tried to imagine hordes of tiny salmon struggling in the mile and a half of upper river we fished, and failed.

"What's it like?" I asked. "Do the fry come down in a big glut, or what?"

Ejnar cleared his throat. "I hope you see it. A fair hatch will keep the river lively but sometimes a great quantity come. Then the river goes mad. Leaping, slashing trout everywhere. It's unbelievable."

"And yet they can be unbelievably hard to catch," remarked Cecil Brown, rising to leave. "As you'll no doubt find out."

Next morning we went off in the boat by ourselves in what was to be a series of long skirmishes with the trout, which, by the way, were not ordinary rainbows but the famous Kamloops of British Columbia, noted for their extreme agility and size. Because of this, they have been stocked in many places far from their original Kamloops lakes. It is this strain that stirred such excitement at Lake Pend Oreille in northern Idaho a few years back, when anglers began catching them over 30

Author landing a rainbow on the Babine River.

pounds. Here in B.C., the largest of which I can find a record is a 52½-pounder from Jewel Lake.

"Our best was a 22-pounder," Cecil had told us. "But it came from the lake. They're not nearly as big in the river."

"Just the same, you might see a Kamloops that will surprise you," Ejnar had remarked. As it turned out, Ejnar was a prophet. . . .

A mist swirled over the river that first morning. Trout splashed, though not in the numbers of the evening before. An excitement took hold of me as the boat swung to the anchor and we prepared to fish for the closest risers. Perhaps "chasers" would be a better term, for the trout were driving upward at inch-long salmon fry a few inches beneath the surface.

I picked a trout and cast to it maybe twenty

Trueblood fishing the Babine in evening. Rises of trout and whitefish show on the dark water.

times, but it kept on showing at the same approximate spot in the river. So I quit it and went to work on another.

Just then Ted's reel gave a short howl.

"Good fish?" I asked.

"Feels like a whitefish, and it isn't jumping."

We had caught several whitefish the evening before, intermixed with the trout. Some were deep-bodied and weighed a couple of pounds—hard-fighting fish, everything considered. And delicious to eat. But when you have your mind made up to buy a Cadillac, who wants a Chevvy?

I glanced back when Ted landed the fish. It *was* a whitefish. He unhooked it and threw it back.

The trout still carried their spawning colors—pink stripe from gill covers to tail, and pinkish belly fins—so that when one of them rolled on the surface you got a distinct flash of pink. That's how we knew which rising fish were trout.

"What fly are you not catching trout on?" I asked presently.

"The blue."

"I'm not catching them on the red."

We were using small, thin flies one and one-quarter inches long, made exclusively for this fishing and available at the lodge. The red had a spot of color at the throat in imitation of a young fry still carrying its egg sac, with mallard wing and silver-tinsel body. The blue resembled a fry that had used up its sac and had a stripe of blue feather down its mallard wing. The flies are somewhat fragile; we'd had several chewed into uselessness the evening before. I wished we'd have the same problem right now.

"Charley Barfield just caught his second trout," Ted remarked. Charley was only 200 yards down the pool from us.

Paul Holland, another guest, was anchored even closer across the pool and as I checked him, his rod became a quivering bow and a rainbow leaped.

What were we doing wrong?

"I'm going to move down on some new trout," Ted said presently. He eased the anchor up and let us drift forty yards.

We started again, surrounded now by four or five actively rising rainbows all within easy casting range. Suddenly I saw a trout splash two, three, four times in quick succession. Just as it completed its fourth surface slash I managed to drop my fly half a yard from the spot.

The trout struck instantly, jumped twice in dazzling style and raced with the river as the reel sirened. Seventy yards from the boat he jumped again and was off. The whole affair was a matter of short seconds.

We fished till dark. Here, at the end of a 12-hour fishing day, Trueblood nets another.

"Nice fish," Ted remarked. "While you're standing there grinning like an ape, unpack the coffee and pour some before I die of misery."

"Did you happen to see the trout I cast to?" I asked, pouring.

"Yep. He rose fast four or five times cleaning up a little bunch of fry. Anytime we can drop a fly on one like that again, I'll bet he grabs it."

Meanwhile, several trout within easy casting distance went splash, splash, splash at irregular intervals. Barfield caught another and so did Holland.

Only 47 to go for Charley, I thought.

I grabbed a gulp of coffee, got my pipe drawing well and picked up my rod. A trout rolled not thirty feet away as I started to cast and it was easy

A slow-moving stretch of the Babine, packed with rainbows in the spring.

to drop the fly a little upstream of the widening rings. I waited tensely. He ignored it. I cast again. Same thing. Then he clobbered another baby salmon. These fish were maintaining regular feeding stations in the river, and we must have been doing a fair job of delivering our flies because we weren't spooking them.

What the devil was wrong?

Suddenly Ted caught one of the persistent fly ignorers. The rainbow leaped magnificently, then rampaged down the river. Now it paused and jumped three times very fast. Off it went again. The mark of years disappeared from Ted Trueblood's face.

"All right," I said finally, hating to ask him. "How did you do it? Did you foulhook him?"

Special flies for the Babine resemble sockeye salmon fry which, migrating downstream in uncountable numbers, are preyed upon by waiting rainbow trout.

"Hell no! He's hooked fair. God, what a jump!"

"Pure luck, then?"

"Pure skill!"

"Horse dung."

"Oh, all right. I used that downstream drift Brown showed us last night. The first time I worked it just right, *bang!* and he was on."

We came to call this technique "Brown's Drift" and I guess I hadn't worked hard at it till now because I hadn't quite believed in it. For the one thing you normally *don't* do in fishing a small streamer is make it speed downstream. Tiny fish in the middle of big rivers usually struggle against the current or drift listlessly with it. But these little sockeye salmon—as I was to see for myself later— actually hurry *with* the current.

A rainbow fights on the Babine, active despite the cold water of spring.

Brown's Drift makes your fly imitate this downstream rush.

You cast across the river or a bit upstream and as your line settles, you flip a few feet of it near your rod tip so it makes a downstream loop or "mend." Then you hold the rod straight out from the side of the boat and keep it there while the cast works itself out.

The current pushing on the line belly near the rod causes the fly to whip downstream—a fishing version of crack-the-whip.

Later, back East, I was to find that this system worked well with nymphs for trout. Hurrying a nymph this way seemed to stir trout that ignored a dead drift. On occasion I've also had good results Brown-drifting a streamer or bucktail, particularly in rising or high water.

Anglers on the Babine about to stretch their legs and have lunch.

When Trueblood finally brought his subdued
Kamloops to the side of the boat—a beautiful
three-pounder—I immediately began casting from
the other side, trying Brown's Drift to the best of
my ability on a trout that had spurned me
repeatedly. I cast five or six times, the tension
mounting as I pictured my fly tempting the trout
at each pass.

Suddenly on the next cast he took it. Off he
went like an arrow downstream. There is a delicious moment just after you've hooked a trout
when you try to assess its size. I judged this one to
be as big as Ted's and when he jumped a moment
later I guessed he was even bigger.

A hidden part of you that has been dead all
winter comes fully alive at a time like this. What
has been a wistful dream is now Technicolor
reality. The reel screams and sobs and chatters. The
strength of David flows in your rod arm. There is
no way to check such a fish; you just hold the rod
and let him run his heart out. I had come a long
way for this thrill. New York to Seattle by
Northwest jet, friend's car to Vancouver, then
north 500 miles on Canadian Pacific Airways to
Smithers, B.C. Now a fifty-mile taxi ride to the
lake. A twenty-mile boat ride to the lodge. Ten
minutes by outboard to this lovely spot. To the
isolation that comes where there are no roads, no
railway, no phone, no TV, no newspapers.

Heaven, with a lusty big rainbow jumping far
down the river and attached to you.

When I finally got him in, I judged the weight at
a bit over 3 pounds before I slipped him back
into the river. My coffee was cold and my pipe had
fallen into the bilge. What trifles! With deep
satisfaction, I picked up my rod and started to cast
again, wreathed in the subtle sweet scent of trout
from the net by my feet.

A trio of harlequin ducks flew up the river

hardly a long cast away. The soft green bloom of spring overlay the hills. There was still plenty of snow on the tops of the nearby Rockies and a big glacier flashed in the sun.

"Ahh!" said Trueblood, onto another Kamloops.

And so a long day, with lunch in the boat, passed swiftly, excitingly. But by evening the river was strangely dead. We headed back for the lodge in the wake of the other boats, pausing once to read the crude inscription on a white wooden grave marker standing starkly alone at the crest of the bank.

"Jenny Holland froze here," it read, "on Nov. 5," followed by an indecipherable date in the 1940's.

On the Babine, many trout leaped eight or nine times.

"Makes you feel cold right now," muttered Ted. "And you know, it *is* cold—I can see my breath."

The thermometer hanging outside our cabin stood at 48 degrees, much cooler than the evening before when the trout had been so active.

At dinner, Charley Barfield was grumbling about the fishing and blaming it on the earliness of the season—we had arrived on May 21st instead of the traditional June 1st. And spring was a little late this year.

"Don't believe I caught more than a couple of dozen," Charley was saying.

A great day, I was thinking, *and I know damned well we didn't catch two dozen between us.*

Next morning it was raining. Ted took the water temperature and found it to be a chill 42 degrees. There was little activity on the river but we knew that droves of trout were there, so we began experimenting. I made one unusual discovery almost immediately, by accident.

My rod was under my arm with the line and fly trailing straight downstream while I got my pipe going. A trout struck, then exploded from the river. The fish was a fine reel-screamer but got off after a flurry of wild leaping.

After that, when we stopped for lunch or paused for any reason, one or both lines would be left trailing in the current. We must have caught half a dozen fish this way. I particularly remember a trout that struck Ted's fly twenty minutes after we'd begun lunch one day. The rod was unattended and out of reach. What a scramble!

But this cold, rainy day was an intriguing one. We tried fishing on the bottom with Wet Cel lines which sink rapidly even in fast water, hoping the trout might succumb to stone-fly nymphs. They didn't, so we returned to the slow-sinking lines which most prefer for this wet-fly work because they put your fly not much deeper than a foot on a long cast.

We explored the river from the top of the first great pool, down past Barfield's Bar, a favorite spot where the pool pinches to a narrows, to Smoke House Island Pool, where the river becomes a big lazy S and enters a small lake. Once in a downpour we beached the boat on Smoke House Island, no bigger than a couple of acres, and took refuge in one of the barnlike smoke houses in which the local Indians cure salmon.

Afterward the sun broke through for about half an hour and the river awoke temporarily. We had gone to the top of the pool because of some activity there when a tremendous trout rolled at the edge of the current.

"My God," said Ted, hauling in the anchor at top speed so he could move us within casting range, "that fish was a 10 pounder or I'll eat it raw, guts and all."

"It was bigger. Twelve pounds, maybe more."

The great Kamloops rolled again.

In my excitement to get a fly to him quickly I forgot about the breeze, making no allowance for it and driving my fly into my coat collar.

But Ted got off a good cast and we sweated out his Brown's Drift together, hardly daring to move as the fly darted along under the surface. Then the trout rolled again, several yards downstream, and we cast again with renewed frenzy.

"Maybe there are *two* big fish," I ventured.

"Wouldn't that be something! Just suppose we each hooked a big one at the same time!"

The sun disappeared abruptly, never to reappear that day, and the river activity dwindled to an occasional rising trout. I had a momentary thrill when I hooked a heavy-feeling fish where the

Ted Trueblood weighs a
husky rainbow on the Babine

whopper had first rolled, but it proved to be only a large whitefish, logy in the cold water, which was still 42 degrees.

At dinner that evening, I overheard Cecil Brown remark, "We saw a trout as big as a beaver today."

I winked at Ted. We knew where *that* one was, unless Cecil had found another. . . .

What makes a fishing trip memorable? Often it is the challenge of the fishing itself, rather than the fish you catch. Somehow the Babine River got a hold on us that was so strong we decided we could not afford the time to go to the lodge for supper for the remaining four days of the trip. We'd eat in the boat.

This held even on our one day of great disappointment when the river was a bare 41 degrees in the morning. That day—and the marks of our score are still penciled on the gunnel of our boat—Ted caught one trout and one whitefish. I caught one whitefish at a few minutes after 10 P.M. We had been on the river twelve hours, not counting time out for a short visit to Fort Babine, which lies above the fishing at the start of the river.

I had never visited a Hudson's Bay Company post before and had high hopes when we entered the white building. A sign inside the door announced that the company's 291st anniversary sale was in progress. I don't know what I had expected, but it wasn't the sort of general store we found.

Perhaps I had expected to see a pot-bellied stove and a leathery-faced old Scot in charge, with a snug cubbyhole of an office and a bottle of Hudson's Bay Company Scotch on hand on a tray with glasses. And bales of furs everywhere. Notions left over from childhood, no doubt.

A young, energetic Scot with a pretty wife ran a spotless store. The remainder of their furs (most had already gone to the Montreal auction) were in the attic—beaver, otter, wild mink, some bobcats, a fisher or two, and piles of tanned moose hides with the hair removed.

Back to the river we went to fish through a long sunny evening. A few trout showed, but we couldn't interest them. Charley Barfield and Paul Holland had long since gone back to the lodge.

"Disappointing, but not a disaster," Ted remarked as I unhooked my only catch of the day, an ice-cold whitefish.

That was the low point of the trip. The high point came on a sunny afternoon when the water temperature reached 49 degrees. We were halfway down the first big pool when the river suddenly came alive.

"Look at those little devils swim!" Ted said, pointing at the water beside the boat. Half a dozen fry in an area the size of my hat were hurrying with the current. Twenty yards downstream of the stern, a trout began slashing at them, we both cast and became entangled.

Now fish rose freely on every side and it was possible to cast to trout slapping at little bunches of fry, instead of to a fish just taking an occasional fry. In five minutes both of us had a leaping Kamloops on, fortunately on opposite sides of the boat.

I gave a hurried glance upstream. Hundreds of fish splashed after fry!

A heavy swirl occurred only ten feet from me as I unhooked my trout. I Brown-Drifted to the fish and he took willingly. It was a whitefish which I hurried in so I could be rid of him and cast to a trout. As it neared the boat, it regurgitated the fry it had just eaten—as fighting fish often will—and as it did so a large trout of perhaps 5 pounds appeared and snapped up the dead fry.

I yelled to Ted, but he was busy with another trout.

I got the whitefish off and went after the big trout but couldn't find him with my fly. A lesser trout took, however, and went bouncing off downstream. When I got it aboard I was surprised to find that it was a cutthroat.

"Now I've seen everything," Ted said. "A jumping cutthroat."

We were to catch several more before the trip was over; thickly spotted, beautiful trout and all of them good jumpers.

"What about the whopper down at Smoke House?" I asked suddenly.

"By God! With all this feed in the river—"

We went roaring downstream, past scores of feeding fish, then drifted into position at the head of Smoke House Pool. A fish swirled heavily in the eddy as the boat swung to the anchor.

I held my breath as Ted's fly Brown-Drifted to it.

Suddenly the reel was screeching as a fish raced with the heavy current. Then a Kamloops of about 3 pounds leaped wildly.

"Did you think of it just then as 'only a 3-pounder'?" Ted asked.

"Yes, that's what this place does to you. Anywhere else we'd be playing a fish like that mighty carefully."

We both fished the area carefully without glimpsing the big trout, then eased on down the pool. Lots of trout were feeding actively and it became not unusual for us to have two on at once. Early in the evening, Charley Barfield, with Cecil guiding, came into the pool and gave particular attention to the big one's corner.

At dusk, they roared off to the lodge and we had the whole of Smoke House to ourselves. The snow-capped Rockies turned pink as the sun set. It was so quiet you could hear trout slap at fry fifty yards away.

The river was no longer wild with rising trout, but there was a good showing of fish just the same. We came to the last stretch of the river beyond the island, where the current smooths out and meets the lake. Several fish were rising quietly and steadily as we went to work on them.

Ted lifted the anchor a final time so we could drift within range of a pair of feeders more in the lake than in the river. We caught them both, played them in the failing pink glow of late evening, released them and wiped our hands on our pants.

I looked around for another trout to cast to. There was none.

"We've educated them all," said Ted. "Let's go back to the cabin and open a bottle of whisky in celebration."

Trueblood netting a trout on the Babine.

I groped around in the bottom of the canvas bucket I carry my tackle in and came up with a bottle.

"You're a genius," proclaimed Trueblood.

We toasted the river and got our pipes freshly filled and going. Then we toasted Cecil Brown and Ejnar Madsen for liking the fishing so much they refused to put in more cabins, fearing a bigger clientele might spoil the river.

A trout slapped noisily upstream, distracting us momentarily.

"We never did catch fifty trout a day, even between us," I remarked.

"Nope."

"And I don't think we're going to catch the big one."

"Nope."

The upstream trout slapped again.

We toasted the superb cook at the lodge, even though we'd only seen her at breakfast lately.

"Just the same, it's been a hell of a good trip so far."

"Damn good. What'll we drink to next?"

I thought a bit. "How about your polar-bear streamer?"

"You're a genius."

We began using this river favorite that Ted had tied in quantity before the trip and had done well with it all day.

A moment later I happened to look downstream toward the lake and saw a trout rise quietly. Then I saw another one.

"Look," I pointed. "They're getting their courage back."

"Courage, hell! They're new fish just coming into the river from the lake."

"When it comes to trout, Trueblood, you're the genius."

We picked up our rods without another word and went to work. If the light held, we'd have at least another twenty minutes.

Cutthroats at 11,000 Feet

AT FIRST IT was just like any ride into Western hills. The horses plodded along a trail that meandered a little above a stream winding among the cottonwoods. A brilliant morning sun flared off the steep, galvanized roofs of a cluster of buildings huddled at the foot of the mountain. This was the last ranch in the valley. Little Red, a pack mule, trotted along jauntily just ahead of me, clanking a bunch of aluminum rod cases. Finally we came to the last gate.

Ahead lay what we hoped would be some unusual trout fishing in lakes of a rugged area of the Colorado high country. We'd brought spinning gear and fly rods, plus all sorts of lures and flies, but for the umpteenth time I wondered if I'd forgotten something vital. From previous experience I knew that timberline trout can be maddeningly picky.

The trail became a series of switchbacks. Far below ran the Los Piños River, which had dwindled to brook size in the twenty miles we'd been following it into the mountains of the San Juan Wild Area. The going soon became so tough that we had to stop the horses after each steep assault to let them blow.

The others—my wife Pris, teen-aged son Steve, and packer Harry Crow—sat their horses patiently. We looked only up now, up to new country, up at the spruces beckoning in the gathering dusk.

The last part of the trip was just a wild scramble as the horses plunged upward in heavy timber. It took all my attention to avoid getting whacked by branches in this upended country, where there are such odd names as Horse Thief Park, Starvation Gulch, Hunchback Pass, Dead Horse Creek. But at last our spirits were raised by the sight of a campfire winking among the trees ahead. A horse whinnied a welcome from somewhere nearby in the darkness.

"This is no place like home, but you'll hate to leave it," Harry Crow said. "Whisky, anyone? Liniment?"

I caught a star glitter on a bit of water at the bottom of a steep slope.

"Elk Lake?" I asked.

"Yep," Harry said. "It's so high they have to stock it by plane."

It was frustrating not to be able to see our surroundings or the lake just then, but perhaps it was just as well, for I'm sure I wouldn't have slept.

When Steve stepped out of the tent next morning, he took a look around and said just one word: "Wowee!"

We were at the edge of a mountain meadow ringed by spruces. Fifty yards north, the ground pitched sharply down in a widening sweep. Horses grazed at the bottom. The little lake lay just beyond in a rocky, evergreen-framed amphitheater. As I watched, trout began to dimple its surface here and there.

But it wasn't just the view. Or the spectacle of the white cook tent, a tendril of smoke from the

morning fire drifting above it. Or the patches of
wild flowers in vivid yellows, purples and reds.
What really stopped me was the utter clarity of the
air at 11,000 feet and the sweet sharpness of it in
the slight chill of a morning late in August.

The high country is an aloof, different world. It
is beyond the tin-can line, beyond telephone poles,
beyond any sign of man save his horses and
temporary tents. Here the wind sings only for you.

And here, we learned, the trout can be different
too. We'd hurried down to the lake after breakfast,
and Steve had gotten a strike on his first cast. He
was spinning, using a minnow-shaped metal lure
with a silver finish.

On the fifth cast, he got another hit and landed
a plump cutthroat about a foot long. But he didn't

Steve (left), Pris, and Harry
Crow arriving at Ute Lake
high up near the Continental
Divide at about 11,000 feet.

take another until a couple of hours later as he explored along the shore.

Meanwhile, I put together a fly rod and walked to the edge of a little beach where there was a rather sharp drop-off. As I stood looking into the clear water, a trout swam up so close that I could see its eyes swivel as it searched for food. I had to stand motionless for perhaps a minute to avoid spooking it.

I tied on a nymph and went to work. Now and then a trout rose nearby, and I saw others cruising the shallows. I would twitch the nymph (now changed from dark to light gray, then to tan) as it sank hardly a yard from a passing trout. No reaction.

"I think their lips are sewed shut," I said to Pris.

Author with a trout at Ute Lake.

She was sprawled in comfort, face tipped to catch the sun.

"Relax," she said. "This is a vacation, not a contest."

"One more cast."

A sudden breeze swept the shore. My cast was a mess. I yanked in line, raised the tip to make a new cast, and felt a trout. Somehow it had plucked the little nymph from among the coils of line, and I was lucky enough to have started my pickup at that instant. The trout made a valiant run or two, dived hard once, then yielded. It was a 14-incher, ice cold and firm, its black spots so pronounced that they looked as if they'd been painted on.

"Caught it by mistake," I admitted. "I must be doing something right, but I don't know what it is."

I'd been casting for an hour, so I flopped down to unwind a little and to admire the trout. Laid on a patch of emerald moss, the fish glittered like an incredible piece of jewelry wrought in two shades of gold—a pale yellow-pink on the belly changing subtly to a light green-gold on flanks and cheeks. The two strokes of crimson under the jaw, trademark of the cutthroat, were vivid. On some I've caught, these marks were faint or missing entirely.

"Is it rare?" Pris asked.

"This one may look special," I said, "but it and the rainbow are the original trout of the West. Out here, people call cutthroats "natives." They range from northern New Mexico, through the West, and clear to the Yukon and Alaska. William Clark, of the Lewis and Clark Expedition, discovered the cutthroat. It's *Salmo clarkii* in case you get on a quiz show, and . . ."

Steve shouted. He'd hooked another across the lake. I could see several trout rising right where I'd been casting. I leaped up, bit the nymph off my leader and even though I'd been using a slow-sinking line, hurriedly tied on the first dry fly I could pluck from the box. It was a large Grasshopper. I excitedly whipped out a cast.

A trout promptly clobbered the fly, and I let out a yell as the fish streaked away. Trout continued to rise as I fought mine, but I could see no naturals on the water. Then the lake went dead calm, and the rise stopped. My trout flashed like a knife blade turning in the sun as I drew it, flopping, onto the beach.

There was no need to hurry. They'd rise again soon, and we'd be ready. I put a floating line on my rod and rigged another rod similarly for Pris. I tossed out the Grasshopper, Pris a Light Cahill.

"We just leave them out there?" she asked.

"That's it," I told her. "Either they'll start to rise again and you can pick a fish to cast to, or . . ."

"Take it. Take it!" Pris urged. A trout had eased up beneath her Cahill so close that the water bulged and the fly rocked. But the fish didn't strike.

"Twitch the fly a little," I suggested. "Maybe the last few inches of your leader are floating."

Just then another trout swung by my fly but wandered away without taking a close look. Off to the right, I could see two more cruising about. The place was beginning to look like a hatchery, and my pulse kicked into overdrive.

Pris swore in an unladylike manner. She'd missed a strike and had hung her fly in a bush.

I could see the bottom clearly twenty feet down, and any fish that swam into the shallows was instantly visible through my Polaroid glasses unless a breeze riffled the surface. But it was the

Harry Crow flours a trout for breakfast as Pris watches.

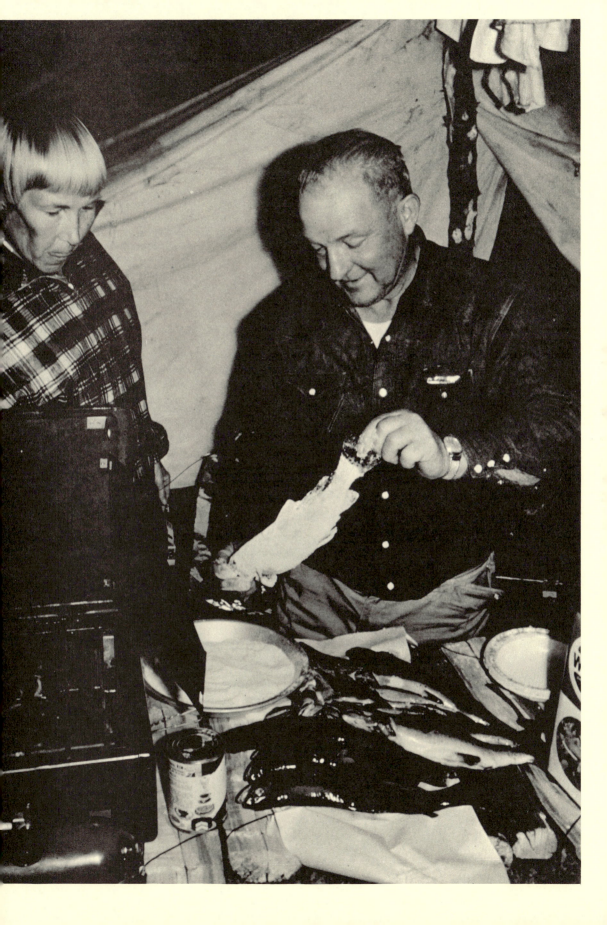

trout out beyond the drop-off that caused the most excitement. One would appear suddenly from the depths swimming toward a fly, and since there was no warning when this would happen, you had to stand there staring at your fly.

After I'd suffered through close inspections of the Grasshopper by three trout, I decided to open up the two we had caught and placed in a pool of a tiny inlet stream nearby. While I was checking their stomachs—there wasn't much there, and none of it was distinguishable—a trout took my neglected fly and of course spat it out quickly.

"One trout on a nymph and one on a dry fly," I said to myself. "Maybe it's time to experiment some more." I switched to a small, gray nymph, waited until a trout swam into the shallows and then dropped the nymph about six feet ahead of

Author about to land a trout at Elk Lake below the campsite.

the fish. It turned the other way. Presently, another cruised near, but I misjudged my lead and almost brained the trout. It fled.

Then I got lucky. The nymph landed a yard ahead of a cruiser, and the trout took, though ever so casually. I got carried away watching the fish fight in that clear water and probably played it longer than necessary.

A bit later, we all began the short climb back to camp. We had five nice cutthroats and a feeling that we'd caught them in spite of a situation we hadn't yet grasped.

Originally we'd planned to drive from our home in Connecticut to Colorado on this vacation trip in August, for we had already been farther west by car—to West Yellowstone, Montana—when Steve was four. That had been our first family campout, and, though it had taken place ten years earlier, I still remembered the long drive. This summer the domestic airlines abandoned the weight limit on baggage and instead offered to accept two generous-size suitcases plus one carry-on piece per passenger. So we flew family plan and saved nine days of travel by car.

In the end, I doubt that the flight was any more expensive than average cross-country car travel, and we didn't have to leave anything necessary behind, though the sleeping bags were sent ahead separately. Some skycaps staggered a bit under our baggage, but the airlines were glad to see us.

We flew to Denver, then southwest to Durango, where Mickey Craig met us and drove us to his Wilderness Trails dude ranch. His address is Bayfield, but the ranch is actually about ten miles to the north, near the tip of Vallecito Reservoir. We made the entire trip in only half a day.

I'd never been to a dude ranch before and must admit I had thought it would be something to be endured. Instead, we found ourselves having a great time. The ranch lies in an unspoiled valley at the foot of the high country in a picture-postcard setting. The Los Piños River flows through the middle of it and provided me with some of the finest dry-fly fishing for browns and rainbows I'd had in years.

But the pack trip was foremost in our minds, and soon we were taking rides into nearby hills to get saddle shaped and to sample the mounts we'd use in the high country.

The pack trip had brought us into another world, and now we had an intriguing trout problem to solve at our leisure. Also, Colorado's early deer-hunting season opened the following day, and we planned to look for a couple of bucks with good racks.

"These Elk Lake trout are temperamental," Harry Crow remarked while preparing lunch. "Sometimes they'll take anything. Maybe you just haven't hit the right time of day yet."

We were sprawled about near the campfire, loafing and watching the hobbled horses. A chipmunk appeared on a flat rock fifteen feet away to clean up leftover oats which Darrell Newton, a Ute Indian who would be guiding us for deer, had spread on the rock the night before for the horses.

I got up and made my third trip to the water bucket since returning to camp. When I remarked on this, Harry said that living at 11,000 feet dehydrates a person. This was the only physical difference from life in the lowlands that we noticed.

"Are there many trout lakes like Elk up here?" Steve asked.

"I could pack you into a fresh lake every day for a couple of weeks," Harry told us. "Now, take Ute, just across the Continental Divide to the northeast, a pleasant ride from here. My wife caught a 6-pound rainbow there one evening. These mountains are full of lakes that seldom see a fisherman."

We certainly had been enjoying seclusion. I glanced down at the lake and saw two rises. I almost got up and ran down to them. Though a cutthroat rarely leaps, the trout in Elk had fought well, and not one was under a foot long. There was another rise. I gulped my lunch.

Soon we headed for the lake to rejoin the attack. Steve, who had never ridden bareback before, climbed calmly aboard his horse and successfully navigated the steep descent. It was a gorgeous, lazy sort of afternoon. Little puffy clouds drifted across the peaks in unending procession. Our "private" trout lake lay before us in sparkling splendor, and the remaining days of our vacation stretched promisingly into the future.

We caught some trout that afternoon, and just

Author playing a cutthroat trout at Elk Lake. Wind blowing insects from nearby evergreens would bring on a frenzy of surface feeding by the trout.

before it was time to pack up I nailed three in a row on dry flies. I thought I had found a feeding pattern at last. But no, it was too simple a solution—surely these trout were more complicated. Still, I resolved to put my notion to the test again as soon as possible.

The chance didn't come until three days had passed. During that time, Steve and I each shot good bucks and helped get the meat back to camp. We'd had several bouts with bad weather, which had come boiling across the nearby Divide, but when I stepped out of the tent one morning, the sky was clear, and there was a skim of ice on the water bucket.

After breakfast, we tied the rods onto Little Red, our mule, and climbed aboard the horses, for

Pris hitches a ride behind Harry Crow up the hill to camp.

this was the day we were going to fish Ute Lake, twelve miles away across the Divide. The three-hour ride was stupendous.

The peaks along the Divide are a Shangri-la, constantly refreshing to the eye. "Look at that rock chuck run!" "There's a pica up on the point watching us!" It was look, look, look. And by now we were so at ease on our horses that we could romp down the steep slopes like gangbusters.

"What's it like to ride on a snow bank?" Steve asked. We had just come to a long one extending for several hundred yards below a rim.

"I'll show you," said Harry Crow. The snow appeared soft but proved hard enough to support the horses. "The snow's usually gone by now," he told us, "but we had a pile of it last winter."

Harry cleans fish, Pris works a fly at Ute, which held rainbows and rainbow-cutthroat crosses to 16 inches.

Later, after a tricky, winding climb among huge boulders, Harry pulled his horse off the trail at a summit and urged us forward. "Gunsight Pass," he announced. We were above 12,000 feet now, but still there were peaks above us. The rooftops of the Rockies fell away into infinity. We crossed the Divide and switchbacked down toward green meadows. Soon we were looking down on the glacial cirque that contained Ute Lake, blue as a gem and obviously deep.

As we were tying the horses to bushes bordering a little inlet stream, I saw a trout rise, then another, and my heart leaped. Pris, Steve, and Harry soon departed with spinning gear and a huge assortment of lures. Ute is about three quarters of a mile in diameter, a bit larger than Elk, so there was plenty of room for all.

Pris and Harry with Ute Lake trout.

I rigged a fly rod with a floating line, 12-foot leader, and a No. 10 dry fly, an Adams. Then I walked to the shoreline and dunked leader and fly in the shallows. The lake was like a mill pond at that moment, so I just stood there watching. Not a trout showed anywhere. The water was shallow for a few yards from shore, then it deepened sharply.

Suddenly, a breeze riffled the surface, and I picked up the rod. As the ripples died, I thought I saw a swirl and made a hasty cast to the spot. The fly floated well.

"Got you," I said out loud to a 14-inch rainbow cavorting in the sunshine. The trout uncorked four magnificent leaps, made a splendid run, jumped again, then began to tire.

The same fly that had worked on three fish in a row at Elk had scored instantly at Ute. So far so good for my theory. I walked downbeach a little way, made a long cast, and propped the rod against a bush. I felt there was no need to fish intently now that the lake was flat calm again. Sure enough, nothing happened to the fly.

I had time to look around. What a spot! The others were well around the lake, casting steadily. Our horses dozed by the stream. Purple wild flowers carpeted the bank nearby. Ute was as clear as Elk and at the moment appeared empty of fish.

But wait till a breeze blew.

This was the key, I was sure. Presently, it began to blow again, and as it faded I looked about for rising fish. There! Too far. I ran along the bank trailing a skein of slack and got off a hurried cast. It was calm again, but I could see a trout coming up to the fly. The fish nipped it daintily, and I tweaked the hook into its jaw. It was a rainbow-cutthroat cross, the telltale marks faint-yellow splashes under the jaw.

Pris came over. "Nothing," she said. "Not even a follow."

"Want to catch one on a dry fly?" I asked.

"You know I'm not the greatest flycaster."

"Doesn't matter. Let's walk down the shore. When the wind blows, I'll cast for you and hand you the rod."

Fifty yards along, we paused and waited for the breeze. When it came at last, then faded, I spotted a riser nearby and tossed the fly at it.

"Get ready," I warned as I handed her the rod.

"Oh my gosh!" She had a nice rainbow. But, pleased as she was, I believe I was even happier, for I had lucked upon what made those trout tick.

The mountain breezes were quite strong. Apparently any good breeze would carry flies and insects from nearby bushes, and when the wind faded, whatever insects it carried dropped to the surface. Up came the trout to feast. It was as simple as that.

I had heard of a "grasshopper wind" causing fantastic feeding orgies on Western lakes, but I'd never experienced one, though I've spent summer weeks on various lakes at about the 5,000-foot level in Idaho and Montana. These lakes could legitimately be considered mountain lakes, and trout cruising the shallows there could be caught on nymphs or wet flies. Occasionally, an evening would bring big May-fly hatches. A lake would boil and a dry fly of the right size and color laid near almost any rising trout would catch it.

Up here, I never saw a May fly or any other fly coming off the water. When the wind died at midday, Ute went dead.

Not a single trout was caught there on spinning gear. "We've caught them at other times on practically any piece of hardware you could throw out," Harry Crow said at lunch. "Maybe it's the lateness of the season or the cold weather we've been having."

It was August 31, and it had been chilly enough for a bit of sleet and even snow to fall briefly. None of us was in shirtsleeves this day.

An angler has to adapt to circumstances, and that's what we did. I wish we'd had some plastic bubbles so that those with spinning tackle could have tossed out dry flies. I'm sure many more fish would have been caught. After lunch a few breezes revealed that a point down the shore was a feeding ground for several trout, and we went there. Some were caught.

Then the breeze blew steadily, and there were no more rises. I rigged up a sinking line and cast a nymph to where trout had risen earlier. They were right on the bottom in about ten feet of water, and every now and then one took. The trout were evenly divided between rainbows and rainbow-cutthroat crosses. None was bigger than 16 inches.

Harry put on a memorable feast that evening

Each leisurely day would begin and end at the cook tent.

back at our Elk Lake camp by dipping the fish in a special batter and frying them to a golden crispness. They fell apart when touched with a fork.

Next morning was sunny, and I could hardly wait to go down to the lake and watch the trout from the vantage point of a cliff near the beach that had been so productive. While I was climbing this knob, Pris made a cast from the beach with spinning tackle.

"Mine!" she said happily, half to herself. "My trout." Often, the first few casts with spinning gear would take a trout or two at Elk. But it was always a brief flurry.

I sat on the highest rock and looked into Elk through Polaroid glasses. Only one trout showed. Then the wind blew. When the lake calmed, I was treated to an astonishing sight. Trout came up

A vividly beautiful high-country cutthroat.

everywhere. Not all rose, for the wind had carried only a few insects from the spruce-lined shores.

It was almost comical. These fish were as conditioned as Pavlov's dogs, which learned to associate food with the ringing of a bell. In this case it was the breeze that roused the trout.

I shook a small spruce next to me, and a small, brown sedge fly fluttered out. This was why the brownish Adams had worked so well. But we were to find that almost *any* dry fly would work as long as it hit the water as soon as a breeze died, for the trout stayed up top and fed for only about a minute.

Perhaps these conditions are not always typical. But they were typical then, and it was a great feeling to get up in the morning and, while brushing my teeth in chill water outside the tent, to glance down at the lake, see a rise or two, and know I could do business with those trout.

Frantic Search for

"The Fly of the River"

THE WATER WAS so cold, my legs soon began to ache inside my waders. I hauled out the stream thermometer that I'd remembered to bring for once and stuck its red bulb beneath the surface— 46 degrees! And no wonder, with every mountain in sight half-covered with snow. As I put away the thermometer my hand brushed a box bulging with dry flies. Right then nothing seemed more incongruous than dry flies in Alaska.

I glanced down the river. Not a rod was bent.

Right then I began to get the horrible feeling that we'd bought a lemon. Four of us had flown from New York to Anchorage, then westward along the Alaska Peninsula and across the Valley of Ten Thousand Smokes to the famous Brooks River—Bob Foreman, who'd been here two years ago, Pete Touart, John Cassen and I. The one thing that was sustaining us newcomers was a mounted rainbow on Foreman's wall at home; the fish had weighed 10½ pounds and he'd caught it right here on a fly.

So we fished and shivered, even though the sun was out. Nobody caught much that first day of exploration. A few rainbows that wouldn't beat 2 pounds; some grayling. Just the same, a head of steam began to build in each of us.

"I'm sticking by the deep runs," Bob Foreman said in the cabin that night. "Any big fish that come upriver will rest in those deep spots." A faraway look came into his eyes.

John Cassen merely nodded. We all knew he wanted a big rainbow to mount and put over his bar at home.

"This may sound cockeyed," remarked Pete Touart, "but I have a hankering to take my spinning rod down to the river mouth first thing tomorrow. I figure I could let a Flatfish float way out into the lake with the current, and then—"

We sat there for a while envisioning that "and then—." If ever there was a place for technicolor dreams, this was it. We were completely remote from civilization and surrounded by beautiful fishing water. Naknek Lake lay sparkling only 50 yards from our door, and the Brooks River rippled nearby. A chill wind keened about the cabin but the little stove purred comfortingly and there was an opened jug on the table. Presently I got to thinking about all the grayling I'd seen in the slough just back of camp. I'd never fished for grayling before, but surely there was some fly that would make them go wild. . . .

The Brooks was slow to give up its secrets but I'll say one thing for it—when it decided to give us a come-on, it was dramatic about it. I can still hear Pete's yell of triumph when he got the heavy strike after letting the current carry his Flatfish 200

Bob Foreman unhooks a big rainbow on outlet river of Nonvianuk Lake on Alaskan Peninsula.

yards into the lake. But the fish proved to be a small lake trout, a major disappointment when you've been dreaming of a yard-long rainbow. He caught another, turned it loose, and then the spot went dead.

Down at the big bend pool, John Cassen was raising his fly rod to make another cast when a huge rainbow came to the surface a moment too late to catch his fly.

My grayling slough was so roughed up by wind that I couldn't tell whether there were still fish in it, so I went on up the river, fishing as I went. The Brooks is only about two miles long and most of it is restricted to fly fishing. A little later in the spring there is a tremendous run of sockeye or red salmon up it. This in turn draws the huge Alaskan brown bears to the river, and I traveled the banks on bear trails. I noticed that all the bars were littered with dried-up sockeye heads. But there was no fresh bear sign; only the splay-footed tracks of a moose.

I came to the famous falls, about eight feet high and spanning the entire river. Here, when the salmon are running, you can see as many as three or four in the air at one time, jumping toward the upper river and its gravelly spawning grounds. But if there were rainbows below the falls I couldn't catch them and I went on.

A quarter of a mile farther I stopped to light my pipe and got the shock of my life. A rainbow came out from under the bank at my feet, followed by another, and paused in three feet of water about a yard away. They were whoppers—fish of about 7 and 8 pounds—and so close I hardly dared blink, let alone move. I could see their black spots plainly, and their reddish flanks. One of the trout snapped its jaws as if savoring some morsel.

After a couple minutes of watching I decided I'd have to try to move away from these fish so I could drift a fly to them or go out of my mind. Backing ever so slowly, I managed to get away without disturbing them and was soon well out in the river. I put on a nymph, located the bush directly opposite the rainbows, and made a careful cast a couple of yards upstream of it. But the trout must have moved a couple of yards upstream, for when the nymph touched the water they took off in wild alarm and that was that. I'd cast right over their backs.

Shaking with excitement, I got out of the river and carefully continued up the bank, pausing often and looking hard. I soon found a solitary fish of about five pounds, then a bunch of them lying together like logs. My heart jumped. A couple of those rainbows looked like 10-pounders!

All but one or two of the dozens and dozens of rainbows caught were returned to the river.

I stared till my eyes watered. Those rainbows were a terrific tonic, because I hadn't quite believed in this trip. For though we were in a wilderness, these waters have been fished a lot. Brooks Camp is operated by Northern Consolidated Airlines, an Alaskan outfit with headquarters at Anchorage. Northern Consolidated has five such camps in and around the Katmai National Monument area and has been operating them for ten years. We had bought their one-week package deal. Trout tourists, that's what we were. Yet here right before me was what we'd been promised—whoppers.

It was nearly lunchtime so I hurried back to tell the boys about this bonanza.

"Trout with shoulders!" Pete exclaimed.

We wolfed our way through lunch and took to

The fly author found in the throat of a dead rainbow and then began fishing with as a gag. Nicknamed "The Picka-loomer," this big black nymph with red tail and rubber-band legs was unusually attractive to the rainbows.

the bear trails. Soon we were gazing at those incredible rainbows and after some coin tossing Bob Foreman got in the river for the first lick at them. He made a good cast but when the fly drifted near the fish they scattered wildly.

Foreman climbed out under a barrage of insults.

But it was the same with the next fish, and the next. Perhaps the shallow water they were in—often no more than two feet—made them spooky. Anyway, in half an hour we'd panicked every rainbow in sight.

"There must be a 'fly of the river'," Pete remarked, "and when we find out what it is we'll mop up."

Still looking for it the next morning, I waded out into the lake with the current to work a big fly rod and a big fly. I got out in the channel till the water was half a foot from my wader top and began to work out a long cast. By the time I had it out where I wanted it I noticed the current had undercut the gravel aound my feet by four or five inches so I stepped to one side. . .onto nothing.

The river grabbed me and in the time it took to make two frantic steps I was carried into the lake, unable to touch bottom. I guess I gave a mighty yell. I don't remember. I looked around wildly and saw no one. Then the current swung my feet up to the surface and I was drifting almost flat on my back. I thought: *You damn fool.*

Luckily I was warmly dressed: long johns, Levis and wool shirt, then a down-filled jacket topped with a knee-length rain parka. I began to kick my feet, hoping to paddle out of the wicked current toward the shallows. I couldn't see behind me because I couldn't see past the wide brim of the Stetson I was wearing.

The water started in at the back of my waders and I thought: *This isn't so bad.* I was fairly comfortable just then and wound in my long cast.

But there was underlying panic that was unpleasant. That water was only 46 degrees, remember.

There was a commotion on the beach and I heard John Cassen shout, "Keep swimming. We're coming."

I heard them moving an aluminum boat over the rocks with much swearing—they were plowing the beach with the anchor and didn't know it. The water I'd shipped now took a giant bite at my vitals.

At last I heard the boat slap the water, then Pete's snarl, "How the hell do you start this motor?" Now I heard the welcome rattle of oarlocks and relaxed a little. The current still had me and I was getting very cold.

"Damn it, you broke the oar!" Cassen shouted. Pete had pushed on an oar as John pulled and it snapped.

If I hadn't been so numb I might have laughed. Paddling frantically, the Marines finally made it to me, sweating like bulls. I couldn't get into the boat but that didn't matter. "I happened to look down the river," Pete said, "and all I could see was your hat and your rod, way out there."

Back in the cabin for dry clothes and a whack or two at the jug, we made what was to be a lucky decision.

"Let's fish in that quiet, shallow slough for grayling," I suggested. "Even if that moose you saw chases us, we can't drown in there."

The slough had once been a horseshoe bend of the river. Now there was only a slight current in it. The lower end fed into a backwater, giving fish free access from the main river. The place was loaded with grayling, some of which looked to be a couple of feet long.

Bob Foreman hand-landing a
trout on Nonvianuk Outlet.

I soon found that you had to cast carefully. The grayling cruised the shallows continually, like foraging bonefish, and it was necessary to make a delicate cast well ahead, but not so far that the small fly couldn't be seen. When everything went just right, a grayling would coast up to the slowly moving fly and turn away quickly with it as if he didn't want any of the others to see what he'd found.

I'd heard all sorts of opinions on how grayling fight. No doubt the fish vary according to water temperature and the *kind* of water they live in. I know this—when I hooked my first grayling in a shallow bay and he scooted for the deeper water with enough power to make a siren of my reel, I let out an admiring yell that snapped Pete Touart's

The outlet of Nonvianuk Lake seen from the float plane that brought us there.

head back 100 yards away. And 30 or 40 fish later in the afternoon I was still getting a charge out of each one.

There is something special about catching a grayling when you can witness the whole performance in clear water. The fish looks like no other with that big wavy dorsal fin. At times when the sun is shining through it, the fish seems to be wearing a mantle of phosphorescent jewels. Somehow they are other-worldly.

And the place did nothing to dispel the illusion. Snow-capped peaks rose all around us. A volcano puffed smoke in the far distance. This is the world's most active volcanic region and the Valley of Ten Thousand Smokes is highly unusual—it evolved comparatively recently.

Back in 1912, a peaceful green valley was suddenly wracked with earthquakes for four days, beginning June 2nd. Incandescent sand surged up through the new earth cracks, melting glaciers and obliterating every tree and living thing in its path for 15 miles. When the searing torrent cooled it lay 100 feet thick over the land and became the Valley of Ten Thousand Smokes..

Shortly afterward, Mount Katmai erupted, blowing most of itself into the sky. Ash up to a foot thick fell on Kodiak Island more than 100 miles away. Ash and dust rose into the stratosphere and veiled half the world, measurably lowering the earth's temperature as far away as Europe and North Africa. Once the third tallest peak of the region, there remains of Katmai today only a hollow stump containing a jade-green lake.

Mementos of the upheavals lie at your feet on the Brooks River. The banks at the high-water mark are lined with pumice rocks so feathery light they float when dropped into the water. On many of the region's beaches you stub your toes on beautiful translucent agates, some a fiery red, some pale as moonstones.

And so you catch a grayling in this wild, strange setting and you immediately think: *Let me catch just one more—*.

Walking back to the cabin for supper, Pete said, "What fish! I'll bet we turned loose more than a hundred."

"At least. I noticed you had one real whopper."

"Oh, you saw that one? He was nearly two feet long."

We all met at the cabin and once again the news was the same—the river had not yet produced a good rainbow for any of us. Bob Foreman had been using double-hook Atlantic-salmon flies of the same size and patterns that had produced two seasons before. John Cassen had tried nearly every wet fly he'd brought. They'd caught some 2

Bob Foreman landing a rainbow, Nonvianuk Outlet.

pounders, but that wasn't what we'd come to
Alaska for.

"I still say there has to be a 'fly of the river',"
Pete remarked.

After supper I decided to show the grayling to
Bob and, wonder of wonders, they were rising!
They'd moved from the slough into a big patch of
adjoining river water that moved at just the right
pace for dry-fly fishing.

It was perfect. Though it was 8 P.M., the sun
was still fairly high and warm on our backs.
Perhaps 40 fish rose in one long, beautiful run. We
separated a little and went to work.

Later I looked over at Bob. He was hunched
forward, sweating out a long cast. In time we'd
either caught or put down every rising grayling.

As we climbed regretfully out of the river I
noticed a 2½-pound rainbow lying dead in the
grass. I peered idly into its mouth and saw a big
dark fly hooked deep in its throat. Soon I'd jerked
the fly loose and showed it to Bob.

"What a monstrosity!"

The fly was a black-bodied bucktail type with
dark-brown top hair or wing, a red tail and three
pieces of rubber band sticking down at the throat.

"Watch your language," I replied. "For a gag I'm
going to give this to Pete as his bona-fide, authentic
'fly of the river'."

We entered the cabin and I dropped the fly into
a small puddle of whisky on the table near Pete.

"Here's your precious 'fly of the river'," I said,
"straight from the throat of a dead 10-pounder."

Pete glanced at the awful fly and turned back to
John. "As I was saying. . ."

By the next morning, we were ready to fish a
new river. We'd flown back to Kulik Camp which
John Walatka of Northern Consolidated Airlines
used as his headquarters and now we were flying
with him across the rotting lake ice to the outlet of

Nonvianuk Lake. Walatka, a bear of a man who has been flying so long he makes it look ridiculously easy, was talking of our chances.

"The ice just moved out from the shore two days ago and the river should be hot. No 10 pounders on the fly, perhaps. But at the mouth you might get one that big with spinning gear. Look at that moose!"

He swerved the plane to fly 50 yards from a passing mountainside. The moose was really legging it.

"Nonvianuk is just outside the Katmai National Monument boundary," he went on, "so you might have company from the Air Force. But hell, not a one of them I've seen can handle a fly rod."

Presently he banked the plane over a wide, green river separated from the ice by a narrow strip of lake water. In five minutes we were on the shore and Walatka was taking off. He'd be back for us in eight hours. Meanwhile, we had a river to explore.

We strolled along the shore with our lunch and gear, picking up agates as we made our way to the late Bill Hammersley's cabin, a wonderful sour-dough affair of weathered logs, scraps of corrugated iron and canvas, and a sod roof. A whitened set of moose antlers askew on a post overlooked his meat cache. As we hurried to get rods put together, I completed the gag I'd begun the night before—I got out a box of eight of the horrible flies I'd bought secretly at camp and passed out two to a customer. "Pickaloomers!" John exclaimed, using a nonsense word we'd bandied about the cabin. Somehow it seemed to fit the fly perfectly.

Exactly what happened next—who caught the first fish, how big it was—is not clear because I have an overriding memory of a great experience of

hn Cassen with the rainbow he kept to have mounted for his den.
oreman is in midstream.

my own. And in a way I hate to tell it, because I've never shot a big-game animal in the eye at 500 yards, got a triple on geese, or achieved the equivalent in fishing, and it seems a pity, almost, to break with this tradition.

But three guys saw me wade to the head of a long pool with the dark blue-green of deep water at its far bank. They saw me make a long cast and if any man was close enough, he may have seen the cause of the excitement that suddenly choked me. I'd put on a Pickaloomer and since it was fluffily dry, the damned thing wouldn't go under. So I gave the line several vicious yanks, making a sorry spectacle of the fly that now was only half sunk.

Suddenly a fish rushed at the fly from 10 feet away. A heavy, churning wake marked the path of the attack. Fish found fly. Angler struck fish.

This rainbow was of a special breed. He was the embodiment of a fond dream—a trout of supreme power, dash and courage. He took me nearly half a mile down the river—a journey of pure delight. And even when he could no longer rip line from the reel, he was a grand fish. I led him to the beach at last, unhooked him, hefted him once and slid him back into the cold clear river.

A 5-pounder on the first cast!

I waded back upstream. Bob Foreman's rod was throbbing. I shouted, "Pickaloomer!" at John Cassen.

He waved. "You already told me four times."

Bob started down the long pool, following his leaping, racing rainbow. Then Pete gave a shout; he'd hooked one too.

Trying to calm down a little, I lit my pipe and just stood there savoring the scene. There were 200 yards of choice fishing water in this pool which

Foreman and good-sized rainbow. Fish weighed from 3 to 6 pounds mostly.

must have been over a quarter of a mile long and about 75 yards wide. A warm sun shone from a cloudless sky and no wind blew to spoil the casting. The gently shelving cobblestone bottom I stood on was easy to wade.

As if to remind me that this was Alaska, a big ice cake came floating down the river. Bob Foreman was now out of sight around the bend and Pete was subduing his fish at the tail of the pool. Five minutes later John's triumphant yell of *Pickalo-o-mer!* drifted across the river to me.

Time to catch another, I thought.

The morning became a riot of rainbows. I've never seen anything like it. That long, flat pool must have been paved with eager fish. By lunchtime I'd caught seven fish between 2½ and almost 7 pounds. Our faces became stiff from smiling; our legs ached from chasing fish and then wading back against the current.

"What a way to die," Pete remarked. "You keep at it till you get a heart attack and then ease yourself into the river with the ice cakes and drift out of sight."

"Casting as you go," John added.

"Has anyone had the guts to try anything beside the Pickaloomer?" I asked.

"Bob is still using a dark double-hook salmon fly, downstream somewhere. And catching the hell out of them, no doubt."

We lay back on the dead grass that gave onto the beach at Hammersley's cabin, munching sandwiches. A backdrop of snow-covered mountains faced us like an unbelievable postcard scene.

"Just think," Pete said. "When we're about fished flat by 5 o'clock we stagger up the beach and here comes Walatka in his plane. We're 10 minutes by air from camp, hot showers, whisky, supper and bed. Yet we're in the middle of nowhere with no problems."

The afternoon proved just as spectacular as the morning. We lost track of the number of rainbows caught and released in the big main pool. For the first time in my life, I found myself becoming impatient with 3-pounders. These were the fish that didn't quite have the steam to get out of the pool and take you down around the bend—trout that in other rivers would have been played with extreme care.

But here at Nonvianuk we let 'em run and jump and put extra pressure on them. The sooner you got rid of a 3-pounder, the quicker you could get fishing again for one twice as big. Or three times as big.

Certain scenes that afternoon found permanent places in my memory. I'd caught a "good fish"—a rainbow that took me out of the big pool and

Fishing the Brooks River— lots of big fish but too scary in the clear water above to catch.

down river to a small, deep bend pool. Pete Touart was fishing in the middle of it.

"Anything good in here?" I asked, keeping my eyes glued to my rainbow.

"Good? Watch this!" Pete said. He cast and a trout struck promptly. Pete gave the fish a jolt, whereupon a magnificent silver-and-pink rainbow shot out into the afternoon sunlight, showering spray. It was a "good" fish, sure. But what makes me remember it was the timing. One cast and *boom!* the fish was in the air, just like an actor coming in on cue.

After I'd worn down my fish and released it, here came John Cassen, face split with a huge smile as he followed a fish into the bend pool.

"Get that damned fish out of my way," Pete shouted with a feigned roughness. He'd hooked another.

But John's fish came boring down on him and Pete had to get out of the river.

"I'm going to kill this fish for my den," John said. "He's strong as a bull and—"

The trout gave a last mighty leap.

"That one's got real shoulders," Pete said, raising his rod high so that John could duck under and follow his trout.

Somehow the two rainbows rampaged around in the pool without becoming entangled. Pete set his free but John carried his ashore and whacked it over the head—a deep-bodied, silvery rainbow more than two feet long and weighing, I'd guess, around 7 pounds.

"We can eat this trout if I get a bigger one," John said, admiring the fish as if he'd never seen a rainbow before. "Did you ever see anything prettier?"

John Cassen with the rainbow
he kept to mount.

The other scene I remember is of Bob Foreman fighting a fish in the big pool while enjoying a cigar. Each time the rainbow leaped Bob emitted a grunt wreathed in smoke and at the height of the fray he was puffing smoke like a volcano—four mighty jumps came in the space of about 15 seconds. . .

Presently Pete Touart caught a whopper. Not a 10-pounder, but the biggest rainbow yet for the party. There was a sort of fish corral of rocks at the shore near Hammersley's, with water about a foot deep, and he put the fish there while considering having it mounted.

This was our second day and we caught about half the fish we had the day before by the time we had to stumble up the cobblestone beach and help John Walatka get his float plane safely into the shallows and turned around. And the Pickaloomer was still *the* fly.

"See you kept a medium-sized one," Walatka growled as he wheeled the plane around over the river mouth. He was speaking of Pete's whopper, destined for immortality on a wall.

We flew on in silence. The ice was breaking up. Kulik Camp shimmered on blue water, only five minutes away now.

"Well, cheer up," said Walatka, mistaking our tiredness for dissatisfaction. "We're having thick steaks for supper."

The following day was our last and we took up positions on the big pool immediately, each at a favorite bit of water. I can't ever recall having higher hopes than I did for those first few casts. The fly straightened the leader nicely each time before dropping into the river and I felt in my bones that each cast was as right as it could be.

ohn Cassen landing rainbow, Nonvianuk Outlet.

Yet not a fish came.

I glanced about the pool. No one had a fish. Perhaps it was the sky; solidly overcast in contrast to that brilliant first day. Or were they sick of the Pickaloomer at last?

Ten minutes later I had a thunderous strike which I missed. Then nothing for 20 minutes. I decided to get out to warm up my legs. Bob Foreman was on the bank rummaging for something in his kit.

"This is going to be a *fishing* day," he remarked.

"How do you mean?"

"We're going to have to work for every trout we catch—work hard, just like home."

He lit a cigar and got back into the river.

I thought: *Just like home, except every trout will be a big one.*

A little bit later, I caught my first fish of the day, a glorious crazy-jumping, mule-strong rainbow of about 3 pounds. I savored every moment of the battle. At home in the East, I might catch one such trout in an entire season. But this was my first fish of the day.

In another hour I'd caught a 5-pounder and missed two strikes. This sobering contrast to the first day was good, I told myself. For fishing as wildly superb as we had first found it is dangerous: you might become contemptuous of ordinarily good fishing.

I tried a variety of other flies. Only the Pickaloomer interested them. This fly-of-the-river business is a phenomenon that does not occur everywhere. Yet there are times and places when one fly pattern will be outstanding, sometimes for just a few hours, sometimes for only a day and occasionally for several. Last March in western

Cassen showing off his big rainbow to Bob Foreman.

Argentina I happened to tie on a Brown Woolly Worm nymph I'd bought two seasons ago at Henrys Lake in Idaho, and that was *it* for a wonderful week...

We ate lunch and talked of individual fish we'd enjoyed, something new for the Nonvianuk. Bob had been far downstream but had found nothing to compare with our big pool.

Soon we were at it again and with such concentration that, incredibly, it was all of a sudden time to go. We made our last casts. Then our last, last casts. Now we picked up our gear, cased our rods and walked up the beach.

"Boy!" said Bob suddenly. He'd picked up an agate as big as a tennis ball. "I'll keep this for a paperweight to remind me of this place."

He didn't really mean that, for this had been a trip with built-in memory joggers: the wonderful grayling fishing at Brooks River; the morning the boys rescued me there; the spectacular performance of the Pickaloomer; and a conservative three-day statistic for the Nonvianuk that someone put into awed words as we stood on the beach and watched John Walatka's plane kiss the water like a swallow—the river where each of us caught his weight in rainbows.

Roadside Lake of

Lion-Hearted Rainbows

"THIS CAN'T BE happening to us," Ted True-blood said. "Not in a lake right on a main highway."

Just then a trout jumped a few yards away—a rainbow as long as my arm; hell, as long as my leg! And the splash had hardly subsided when *two* trout just as big came rocketing out not 30 feet from where we stood in the gathering twilight.

I groaned. It was almost too dark to set up tackle and tie on a fly, yet there the rainbows were. And to make this agony worse, one of our party was already fishing with tackle he'd brought completely set up. He was Ray McPherson, fly tier, rod builder and tackle-store operator from Kamloops, British Columbia, some 30 miles north of where we stood.

With deceptive guile Trueblood said, "Let me try that new glass rod you were telling us about, Ray."

A moment later Ted had made a long cast and said of the rod's casting ability, "Man!" Soon afterward he brought the rod up sharply and said, "Wow, look at that—" The reel drowned out talk.

Ted Trueblood plays a mighty rainbow at Stump Lake in this sequence.
Fish is probably about an 8 pounder but since all but a very few were
returned unharmed, this is just an educated guess. Rings on the water
from leaps the camera did not catch show that this fish jumped more
than the four times shown here.

Then a magnificent trout leaped wildly in the half-light, doubled for the beach, jumped twice more, hardly a rod's length away, and zoomed out toward the deeps again.

When at last Trueblood led the trout into shallow water we crowded around and guessed its weight at about 8 pounds, a rainbow of a lifetime—when it comes to fly fishing in lakes. Ted unhooked the fish.

"You going to turn him loose?" I asked.

"Got to. The icebox is full-up, with all our grub, and he's too big to eat for breakfast."

"Think of it—too big to eat!"

Trueblood looked at the fly on his borrowed outfit. "Don't even know what I caught it on."

"We call that a Halfback," Ray McPherson said, handing me one from his fly box.

Trueblood at the edge of Stump, waiting for a rainbow to cruise by so he can cast to it.

Ted flipped it out again. A few casts later the rod shook to the leap of a trout that looked even bigger than the first. This was too much for us onlookers and when the rainbow threw the fly during a foaming rampage, we broke and ran to unpack tackle. But the magic time had passed.

A loon cried on the dark lake as we filed into the camper. I broke open a jug.

"In Maine they say a lake with loons on it is lucky," I remarked.

"Well, Stump Lake isn't lucky," Joe McKinnon said flatly. "It's British Columbia's mystery lake."

"What's the problem?"

"Why, to catch trout with some consistency. They've put about three quarters of a million rainbows in here—fish that weigh up to 18 pounds and more—and most of the time no one can catch any."

"This was to be a showplace lake," Ray put in. "There was a three-day derby when it was opened to the public on May 20, 1961. Fifteen hundred fishermen knocked themselves out but the catch was very small."

"So we hardly bother with the lake," Joe said. "There's too much hot fishing nearby where you can take rainbows up to 12 pounds and more on the fly."

Soon afterward Joe and Ray left. On the table lay a small pile of the best local flies that McPherson had tied up for us. Except for a young couple in a camper nearby, we were alone on a lovely wilderness lake—or so it seemed—except for that road.

The prospects were superb. The *best* lakes in the U.S. and in most of Canada that are reachable by car give fair fishing for brook, brown or rainbow trout up to about 2 pounds. A 3-pounder makes your day and a 5-pounder sets off cries of delirium.

Puffing at his pipe, Ted no doubt had this in

mind when he remarked, "A public lake stuffed with tremendous trout and no one bothering them—who ever heard of a deal like that before?"

I'll never forget the next morning. The lake was a mirror reflecting fir-clad hills. Brushing my teeth, I strolled the few yards across the beach and was nearly paralyzed by what I saw. I beckoned urgently to Ted.

"My God! It looks like a hatchery for monsters!"

Droves of huge trout cruised the sandy beach in barely a yard of water.

"Not a trout under five pounds," I said in awe. "Look at that one over there—he must go ten easy."

"You're being conservative."

Reluctantly we decided to eat, for when Trueblood and I get wound up over fish we may not stop for ten, twelve or even fourteen hours. Once we fished for 24 hours with only a short afternoon nap and an occasional sandwich. So we go in for sturdy breakfasts just in case. Back in the camper, we gulped pancakes and stared out the picture window through glare-cutting Polaroid glasses at the parade of monster rainbows.

"People go all the way to New Zealand and South America to prospect for trout like these," I remarked.

I was thinking how accessible Stump Lake is, 30 miles south of Kamloops on Route 5 in lower-central British Columbia. Kamloops is less than an hour's flight from Vancouver and the lake itself—about 140 miles due north of the U.S.-Canadian border—is only 350 miles by road from either Seattle or Spokane. The lake is five miles long and a mile and a half wide.

Author landing a 12½-pound rainbow from Stump.

"Something tells me this isn't going to be as easy as it looks," Ted said as we quickly got our gear and headed down to the beach.

He was right. Trout were so thick at this south campground that picking one to cast to was a problem because they were all as skittish as could be. A line falling lightly near a trout would cause it to bolt and start a chain reaction of fleeing, panicked fish.

But such trout scarings didn't seem to matter—where four fish bolted, a dozen more would drift by soon afterward, tantalizingly close. And shrewdly close-mouthed.

An entrancing hour passed swiftly with neither of us interesting a trout.

I laid my rod down and lit my pipe. Despite its unromantic name, Stump is one of the loveliest lakes I've ever fished and it was a pleasure to just stand there and look around. The lake lies in hilly ranch country at about 2,500 feet, with firs and some huge yellow pines lining the nearby western shore. But the place had a special look about it that I've noticed elsewhere in the Northwest— maybe it's the clear air, the distant sagebrush on far hills, the ultra-clear water that makes something floating on it seem to be suspended in air.

Ray McPherson had driven me down from Kamloops and all the country was like this; timber, grassland and sudden sparkling lakes. Most of the water I saw was on private ranches but a British Columbia law requires landowners to provide public access to all but small ponds.

The sudden splashing of a large rainbow almost at my feet jolted me back to thoughts of fishing and I decided to try a couple of feet of quite thin monofilament on my leader end. The thinner the leader end, the harder it is for a trout to detect it. Then I tied on a small gray nymph, the tenth or eleventh of my offerings so far.

A trout came swimming along—not one of the

biggest but a breathtaker just the same. I cast ten feet ahead of him and when I thought he'd see the little nymph, I gave it a seductive twitch. The trout took so casually I almost missed seeing the slight opening and closing of its mouth.

The fish felt as solid as a tree when I struck. Instantly the leader end broke. It only tested three pounds. I don't think that trout knew it had been hooked, for it continued on slowly with my nymph buried in its jaw.

That shook me.

If a 7- or 8-pounder could break me so effortlessly, what about a 12-pounder? What about a 15-pounder? I bit back the leader so it now ended with a five-pound-test strand, tied on the big Halfback fly (for the third time) that Ray

The author wanted to catch a trout "as long as his leg" and this was it, the 12½-pounder from Stump.

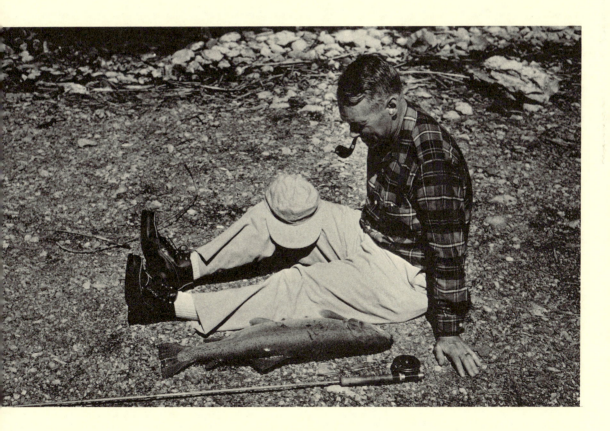

McPherson had given me and went looking for new trout.

I found them 200 yards away at the end of an old dock that belongs to the closed-up copper mine whose lifeless buildings look down on the lake from a bluff. There are half a dozen boats for rent—the only ones on the lake—from the mine caretaker. The crude dock ends with two big logs a yard apart poking ten feet into the lake.

Below the logs—wow! I crept out to the last plank and tried to look as innocent as a dead tree just as a rainbow, about 11 pounds, came swimming out from under my feet. Then here came its twin. And finally another a bit smaller. I felt like a burglar about to rob an all-glass bank.

It seemed impossible that they wouldn't see me

The only "bright" trout taken was this rainbow of about 10 pounds caught by Ted Trueblood, so big we had to cut steaks from it for cooking.

as I lowered the rod and dangling fly ever so
slowly. This was country-boy fishing for trout
above and beyond the size that come in dreams.
*Get the fly on the bottom four feet down and
show the pretty fish the fly whenever he swims by.*

For ten agonizing minutes I did this without
spooking them. It was hard to see the dark fly
against the bottom sometimes, and I'd lose track of
it now and then. So when I noticed the smallest of
the trout working its jaws as if chewing a tasty
morsel, it was a moment before the thought struck
me, *He's chewing on your fly!*

I jerked the rod, felt the fly sink home. The
rainbow went out of there like a Roman candle.

When the trout was 100 feet out in the lake
and jumping wildly, Trueblood came running.
I guess I must have yelled.

"What's he feel like?"

"Like a runaway bus."

This trout was a gentleman. He didn't dive to
the bottom and ram his head into the weeds; he
didn't dash through the shoreline brush; he didn't
roll up on the leader or indulge in any of the
crudities of desperate big trout. He ran and leaped
and ran in the open lake till drugged with fatigue.
Finally I was able to draw him alongside the dock.

Then, while fooling around with pictures, the
hook suddenly came out and he sank slowly in the
clear water.

"Probably just as well," I said a bit shakily. We
still had an overstuffed icebox but I'd like to have
hefted him just once.

"Looked like an 8-pounder," Ted guessed.
"What did you catch him on?"

Here is a sweet moment for any angler. You've
been thwarted by trout you could almost kick out
onto the bank all morning and your partner has to
ask what finally worked.

"The same fly you used last night," I said. "He

mouthed it like a guy chewing on an old cigar.''

Back at the camper for lunch a bit later, we watched the spectacle of the horde of rainbows through the picture window. It still amazed us—those trout within walking distance of the campsite.

"The poor devils," Ted remarked. . . .

To explain that, I must give the background of Stump Lake. I first heard about this fabulous spot from Mike Cramond of Vancouver when he visited New York one April. What he told me seemed impossible, but careful checking proved him right point by point.

The B.C. Fish & Game Branch of the Department of Recreation & Conservation wanted a showplace lake with terrific fishing on a main highway. Who wouldn't? They selected Stump after a careful study and poisoned it on September 9, 1957, to kill off its entire fish population. (The population was mostly "coarse" fish such as carp, suckers, squawfish and—this name kills me—peamouth chub.)

The poison was Toxaphene, actually a cattle spray. Rachel Carson would have called Toxaphene a "bad" poison because in strong concentration it is a total eradicator of life. But Stump, comparatively shallow, was ideally suited for a mild dose of Toxaphene, which at the rate of only one to 100 million parts of water knocked out the fish and the shrimp (a small crustacean quite different from the ocean variety) but not the insect life.

The lake was allowed to clear for two years, then plantings of young rainbows began late in September, 1959. Some of the fry were incredibly small: 630 to the pound. That fall 201,000 trout went into Stump, and it was also restocked with

Ted Trueblood and his "bright" (silvery) rainbow. All the others wore colorful red stripes down their sides typical of trout ready to spawn.

Trueblood turns loose about a 7-pounder. Fish of this size were caught so often that after a time we didn't even bother to photograph them. Elsewhere, every such trout would be a dream trophy.

shrimp. Because of the great amount of other feed in the lake besides the shrimp—snails, leeches, May flies and other insects—the trout gorged and grew prodigiously.

A 14-pounder was caught in Stump in October 1962, on a trolled Doc Spratley fly; and an 18-pounder the following April. My friend Doug Robertson of Kamloops caught a 14-pounder the spring before our trip.

And now we come to Trueblood's remark, "The poor devils."

Those big trout crowding the shoreline wore the gaudy pink stripe and golden sides of spawning rainbows . . . only rainbows cannot spawn in a lake; they *must* have running water and Stump has neither inlet nor outlet. Nevertheless they tried, and dug "beds" in the gravel and among the rocks.

There was something pathetic about these big fish trying unsuccessfully to spawn. But soon they would give up and disappear into the depths to join the host of rainbows not yet mature. Meanwhile they provided visiting anglers with a temporary bonanza.

Or did they?

Those trout nearly drove us nuts. It was like fishing in a hatchery of whoppers with lockjaw. We worked on them for thirteen hours that first day. I'll bet I cast 10,000 times without another strike. Finally in late afternoon Ted caught and released a 6-pounder.

He mopped his brow. "All day for one trout, but it was worth it."

A few hours later, with no more success than a fish each for the day, we walked wearily to the camper in the twilight, washed up outside and stepped inside to deluxe quarters. Or so it seemed

Trueblood casts a tiny nymph to trick a big rainbow cruising by in the shallows.

to me, for till then I'd always camped under canvas. But here were a stove, refrigerator and overhead lights all operating on bottled gas from an outside tank. There was a sink with its own water supply. Bunk beds. Cupboards. A dining table with banquettes. It was neat.

We now fell into a ritual that has evolved from long association, for our camping trips in the West together now total up to many months. I uncorked a bottle of whisky and threw the top over my shoulder, paying no attention to where it landed. Done outside, Trueblood calls the act of refreshment "looking at the stars."

We looked at the stars a few times in the camper.

"What's for supper?" I said presently. It is Barrett's Law that Ted is cook and I am dishwasher, wood hustler and water carrier.

"A damn big porterhouse. Salad. Bread and butter. I dare you to ask for dessert."

Trueblood is a superb camp cook. His blueberry pancakes would make a French chef cry with envy. Once he prepared some neck meat from an old bull elk I'd shot only three hours earlier—still so fresh I doubt it had cooled—and it was so tender you could have cut it was a stick.

Presently pipe smoke and the aroma of the cooking steak blended in the cabin. I laid aside my fly-tying stuff after turning out several fat-bodied nymphs that I hoped would prove chewy to the trout.

The steak was delicious. As for the nymphs, they were to bring some pleasant surprises.

Stump Lake gave up its secrets slowly. Though we'd fished hard but as unobtrusively as possible for its trout, we didn't realize how touchy the rainbows at the south campsite were until a young couple set up camp nearby. The fellow saw the trout and immediately went after them with a spinning outfit and a big yellow Flatfish lure. He soon hooked a big trout that got off after one leap.

A few desperate hours later, still fishless, he launched a small cartop boat and with his girl trolling rowed back and forth over the fish. On the third pass I remarked that he'd soon drive the trout away and he quit immediately. But the damage was done—the fish left and never returned during the rest of our week's stay.

That afternoon Ray McPherson and Joe McKinnon met us and showed us new waters at the far end of the lake where there's a small island. Signs proclaimed that the tip of the lake was temporarily closed to fishing.

"They've been netting trout here and taking their eggs," Joe explained. "Got a million or so last year but only about 60 percent hatched. I hear it was the same this spring."

The Fish & Game Branch had also tried two schemes here to create moving water in the lake. The year before, a huge pumping arrangement created an artificial stream effect. Then paddle-wheels in two large enclosures were tried. But neither procedure prompted natural spawning.

We saw no trout at the island shoals and decided to try what local Canadians call "mooching"— drifting in a boat while trailing a fly with a sinking line like a WetCel or, when becalmed, casting the fly and retrieving it slowly close to the bottom. Either way, you fish blind.

Just as we were about to quit—bingo!

An unseen trout seized Ted's trailing nymph, jumped magnificently once near the boat, then lunged down the open lake. The wonderful sirening of that reel was the first we'd heard all day and it went on and on.

"He's as strong as a bull," Ted said presently, "and he's going to break off if I don't follow him right now."

He yanked the outboard into life and took off in pursuit, reeling for broke. That rainbow was all heart. Twenty minutes later when Ted tried to net it—the trout was so big he had to make four attempts before he crammed it into the net—the fish was nearly dead.

And what a trout! Silver bright on the sides, all muscle.

"If you throw that back—no more whisky," I said. "What's he weigh?"

"Ten and three quarters!"

"Did you ever catch a bigger trout in a lake on a fly?"

"Never. And I've seldom fished so long in a lake for one trout."

This was the mystery of Stump—how could a lake so filled with trout give up so few? Ted's fish, some of whose steaks—as pink as any salmon's—we enjoyed at dinner, was what Joe and Ray called "bright" as opposed to the more colorful "dark" rainbows we'd seen trying to spawn near the shore.

"We're trying to line up a good skindiver to go down and find out where the devil the fish are," Joe said morosely. "Except for a short time after ice-out in April, and again in late September and October when most of us are hunting, you seldom see a trout. Or catch one."

The talk turned to other lakes and places. And as these two Scots-descended Canadians talked, I began to get a picture of two guys living in a fish-and-game paradise so bounteous it was driving them slightly nuts.

McKinnon, who is in the plumbing and heating business, keeps a boat atop his truck all the time, and tackle inside it. "When I leave the house in the morning," he said with a sly grin, "there's no telling whether I'm going to check out a job or a lake. But somehow we get the work done."

McPherson, who has a tackle store in Kamloops, said frankly, "I went broke once because of the fishing. Couldn't leave it alone and my business went to hell. But I've got it under control now—I think."

Partly because of the wind, we never did solve the mystery of how to catch Stump Lake's bright rainbow. I have never seen such a blowy place; Stump could become unsafe for a small boat in a matter of minutes and remain so for hours. When it was just windy enough to navigate we tried trolling flies, and when the wind dropped to a mere breeze, we mooched. But not another bright trout struck.

However, we did put to rest a notion of our Canadian friends that dark fish were hardly worth fishing for. Perhaps they unconsciously associated Stump's trying-to-spawn trout with Pacific salmon, all of which die after spawing and in their final highly colored stages are eaten only by bears, eagles and other scavengers. But rainbows seldom die after spawning and in the U.S. their spring spawning run is *the* event of many a river, especially in the East.

I remember a morning when we discovered a bonanza of dark rainbows snug against a fir-hung bank. For once it was perfectly calm as we eased along about forty feet offshore in the boat. I stood in the bow and soon saw a light-colored area about six feet across where rainbows had scoured the rocky bottom clean—another fruitless spawning bed. And then I saw the fish—5 of them!

Excitedly we anchored in water so clear you could see the color of the trout 25 or 30 feet away. You could actually follow your nymph as it sank slowly, then came to life in little pulsating darts as a huge trout passed nearby.

"He's turning! He's following! He's—"

Ted's suddenly taut rod caused a watery explosion as a big rainbow leaped violently a yard from shore. The trout jumped cleanly three more times, then took off in a sizzling run.

"Nothing sick about that trout."

"No, sir! Color him lively."

In the next hour or so we took 4 trout in that one spot and released them, for if we'd kept them we'd have been finished for the day (the limit is 2 a day when they're 20 inches or bigger, as these were). We guessed their total weight at 30 pounds.

We decided later that the campsite fish that gave us such a hard time were unusually spooky because of the number of people who immediately saw them and went to work on them. Elsewhere, though the trout were seldom pushovers, they would take a properly presented nymph—almost *any* nymph, even an orange one I made up so I could see it on dark days.

And we had some dark days; one so windy it was too dangerous to use the boat. Low clouds raced past just above the treetops, followed by a veil of sand whipped off the beach into the trees. We decided to explore the west shore on foot in case we'd see a trout to cast to in a calm spot.

So far as fishing went, it was a wasted morning. But hiking through the firs put into focus a thought about Stump that had been tugging for recognition: The lake is wild and waiting to be discovered. One thinks of a lake beside a highway as a place whose shores have been trod by countless people, yet we found a primitiveness that only accompanies isolation.

Once we surprised a pine squirrel chasing the devil out of a chipmunk. For fun, I think. They stopped like people caught in an act of foolishness and regarded us gravely. The chipmunk advanced tamely till he was only a yard from my boot. Then with a flirt of his tail he was gone in a whirl of leaves, the squirrel hard after him and scolding like a housewife.

We found a tremendous beaver lodge, maybe fifteen feet across and almost as high above the water, deserted now, and no wonder—the small supply of aspens had given out and the beavers had taken to cutting down firs and stripping their bark.

"I never heard of beavers eating evergreens before," Ted remarked. "Do you suppose they had a halfwit leader who brought them here?"

Later we climbed straight up the hillside and came upon a group of abandoned plank buildings that probably housed the men who worked the old copper mine not far beyond. Two fat rock chucks sat on the steps of the weathered cookhouse in the day's first sunlight, unafraid. A crow cocked its head at us from atop a barn. There was a haunting, wild flavor about the place that bespeaks the odd seclusion of Stump Lake. . . .

Just what is it really like to catch the big rainbows of Stump? I found it a lot like a big-game hunt where one sees so many animals you can pick and choose among them for a good trophy, and then stalk and eventually outwit it. I got the same tremendous lift from catching one of these dream-size trout as I have from shooting a buck—and the same lingering memories of the details.

We automatically thought of each trout as "he," though we actually caught far more females than males. If we saw half a dozen trout in one spot, we'd always try for the largest even if he seemed uninterested in the fly.

A "he" fish that really made the trip for me was a hulking rainbow I hooked in a bay about 300 yards wide. I was casting from shore.

"He's as long as your leg!" Ted said from behind me when the fish swam past, only a few yards away. (Ted was watching, since we fished this little bay alternately so the supply of trout would last longer.)

When the rainbow felt the hook he took off with driving power. You can only let such a fish go where he will. You hold the rod high with the reel free to run and wait for the trout to stop its first panicky dash. But this one never stopped and finally I ran for the boat at the other end of the beach.

"How far has he gone?" Ted asked as he shoved us off and hastily cranked the motor.

"Nearly 300 yards. I'm about out of line."

We soon found that the rainbow had gone around every prominent snag in the bay. But miraculously the line kept coming clear, even when we came to a sunken tree.

"He'd have broken you for sure if you hadn't run for the boat," Ted said. "Is he still on?"

"Stop the boat and let's see."

The line kept going out inexorably and away we went again in pursuit. Now we found he'd traveled the entire length of a reed bed only a yard from shore. Then around a stump and back the way we'd just come.

Twenty minutes later we suddenly found ourselves in the open bay with the fish only fifty feet away yet still powerful. But now it would just take time and a bit later I had him.

He was gulp-sized.

"Hurry to shore so we can get some pictures, then I'll turn him loose," I said, keeping the trout in the net and in the water.

But he'd fought his strength out and couldn't revive in the shallow water by the shore so we had no choice but to keep him. I got out tape measure and scale—at 29 inches he *was* as long as my leg, and weighed 12½ pounds. I was as excited as if I'd just caught a mighty salmon, and as pleased.

There are picnic tables at this little bay. We went over to one and opened a couple of beers. It was a lovely day in early June and for a while it wasn't windy. We just sat there, sipping beer, talking about my trout and looking at it glistening in the shade.

Across the lake, sunlight glinted on the chrome of a passing car.

"They ought to put sedges in Stump so the trout

would have an annual feeding spree on top," I said. "Then almost anyone could harvest these whoppers."

A sedge is a winged aquatic insect missing from Stump, though it's present in nearby lakes. They hatch locally in early June and in such quantity they drift in fluttering windrows on the surface. Trout gorging on them are easy to catch then.

"It would be too dangerous," Ted said. "Think of the car crashes as guys on the road saw 15-pounders wallowing like hogs!"

He picked up his rod and walked to the shore, then eased forward in a half-crouch, his eyes on a big rainbow finning in only two feet of water. We were to catch and turn loose over 30 of these great fish before we just plain lost track of the count.

Trueblood made a cast.

The trout in this bay were scarcer than when we first found them; gone back to the depths probably, where they'd become "brights" again. Meanwhile, from early spring through mid-June, the dark rainbows await anglers in this amazing, passed-by public trout hole.

Trueblood struck a fish and the lake exploded. All we'd learned fishing nymphs at Wade and Henrys lakes was paying magnificent dividends, but the greatest joy was in stalking those big trout one by one, guessing how far to lead each fish, then waiting in an agony of wonderment as the tiny nymph settled in the clear water.